THE
BEHEADING
AND OTHER TRUE STORIES

THE
BEHEADING
AND OTHER TRUE STORIES

BOB CREW

metro

Published by Metro Publishing
an imprint of John Blake Publishing Ltd
3 Bramber Court, 2 Bramber Road,
London W14 9PB, England

www.johnblakepublishing.co.uk

First published in hardback in 2003
Published in paperback in 2011

ISBN: 978 184358 345 5

British Library Cataloguing-in-Publication Data:

A catalogue record for this book is available from the British Library.

Design by www.envydesign.co.uk

Printed in Great Britain by CPI Bookmarque, Croydon, CR0 4TD

1 3 5 7 9 10 8 6 4 2

Papers used by John Blake Publishing are natural, recyclable products
made from wood grown in sustainable forests. The manufacturing processes
conform to the environmental regulations of the country of origin.

Every attempt has been made to contact the relevant copyright-holders,
but some were unobtainable. We would be grateful if the
appropriate people could contact us.

To the memory of Lord Crewe, the deceased Liberal peer
who was opposed to a unified Saudi Arabia – 'what we want is not
a united Arabia, but a disunited Arabia split into principalities' –
whose former London home (Crewe House) has become, ironically,
the Saudi Arabian Embassy.

Contents

INTRODUCTION

This is a second edition of *The Beheading and Other True Stories*, the first of which was published eight years ago in February 2003, and it is being republished in 2011 in response to popular demand, chiefly in Britain, the United States and Europe.

Since I first wrote this book, Saudi Arabia has not moved on with regard to its barbaric laws and savage punishments, with which I am chiefly concerned in these pages, which is why my original twenty-three chapters from the first edition do not need to be updated eight years later, given that they are as relevant and true of Saudi Arabia today as they were when I first wrote them.

They are still relevant because virtually nothing has changed with regard to savage beheadings and other barbaric punishments in the desert kingdom, or with regard to substantial improvements in human rights, gender equality, or the position of foreign diplomats and journalists either. So nothing, alas, needs to be updated.

Just as importantly, the first edition of my book has now become a pioneering historical document for a period of time in recent history that stands for all time, the first of its kind back in 2003, and is still the only publication of its kind on the subject of Saudi Arabia, detailing where the desert kingdom is coming from in the modern world, together with my own personal experiences and eyewitness accounts of it. So this is another reason for not updating or altering the original text, and I shall return to this subject at the end of this introduction.

Essentially, Saudi Arabia is of the same ancient mindset as previously and not least with regard to its women and those who break its laws, the lack of freedom of its citizens and its press, and the precarious position of its foreign diplomats, all of which are the primary concern of this book. Changes that have taken place in Saudi Arabia during the past eight years – such as the streamlined urban architectural landscape, educational, parliamentary and some reported electoral changes – are not and never were the original subject of this book, the overriding concern of which is the lack of human rights progress, including rights for Saudi women, the beheadings and other related stories, which are not to be erased from history just because they were first published eight years ago, and especially when they are still in evidence today.

Currently, a married Saudi Arabian princess has been given asylum in Britain – as reported in the *Daily Mail* (July 2009) – having had an illegitimate child by a British man, and she has been given her asylum on the very convincing grounds that she could and very probably would face death by stoning for her adultery back in Saudi Arabia (see chapter two in these pages on the subject of stoning adulterous women to death). So no change here then:

ditto beheadings, as we know from Ali Hussain Sibat being condemned to death for fortune-telling and alleged witchcraft in Saudi Arabia in 2010, for which he may or may not be reprieved as campaigners try to rescue him (Saudi Arabia reportedly carried out 166 executions in 2007 and 39 the previous year). These are all matters of current concern in the outside world (as well as in more liberal-minded and civilised circles inside the desert kingdom, not that anybody listens to the liberal-minded there!). With some 2,907 views on YouTube about Saudi beheadings, at the last count, the strength of public feeling is all too obvious.

There has also been no change with regard to blood money, lashings, floggings and hand amputations either. See *Middle East Online* (2010) which argues that it doesn't do any good 'lashing a doctor for a claimed wrong prescription' or 'lashing a female teacher 100 times in public and in the presence of her pupils.' How far beneath human dignity is all this? Surely it is finally time for Saudi Arabia to grow up and become more humane.

The Saudi Princess's asylum in 2009 was given to her six years after the publication of my book and, incredibly, the *Daily Mail* tells us that her initial request was turned down because her story was not at first believed to be consistent by the authorities in the UK who also thought that she exaggerated her fears of death by stoning for adulterous women back in Saudi Arabia – the mind boggles!

When people in Britain who should know better choose not to believe – or to ignore – these ugly realities in Saudi Arabia from which they are safely removed, it is hardly any wonder that such heartless and grisly matters also get ignored and denied in the desert kingdom itself.

Of course, Saudi Arabia is the world's largest oil exporter and a welcome ally in the war against terrorism, but this doesn't give it the right to expect Britain's blessing when it stones its women to death, or to expect that Britain will not give asylum to a Saudi woman in danger of being stoned to death. Not that our diplomats or rulers will openly make waves on this account, given that there is so much at stake, including the usual big business deals, of course. We cannot expect our diplomats or rulers to rattle Saudi Arabia's cage in a good cause. Only investigative journalists and authors with fire in their bellies can be relied upon to do that.

Other things that have not changed in Saudi Arabia, with which my book is concerned, include the right of women to drive cars, same as men in the desert kingdom. At the time of writing, Saudi women are still trying to get the ban lifted on the prohibition against their driving cars (see chapter eleven in these pages), and lactating Saudi mothers are doing this by threatening – would you believe? – to breast feed strange men who want to be their drivers, so that these men can drive the family cars that Saudi women are themselves not allowed to drive!

This is according reports coming out of Saudi Arabia in 2010 from *Gulf News* and elsewhere to the effect that breast milk kinship is considered to be as good as a blood kinship in the 'land of the pure.' What this is supposed to mean is that, if Saudi lactating mothers breast feed unrelated men who want to drive their cars for them, these men become family members by reason of – the mind boggles yet again – having taken milk from the breasts of those mothers, enabling the men to mix freely and legally with such women in order to drive their cars for them.

Once the breast milk has magically transformed strange men into the sons of Saudi mothers and the brothers of their sisters and the blood relatives of their daughters, these Saudi mothers – who are otherwise not allowed to mix with men outside the family – can employ these men to drive their cars for them and the other female members of their families. But how much better it would be if Saudi women were simply allowed to drive their own cars, in a new equality with men.

In order to get the ban lifted on their driving, Saudi mothers are now reportedly trying to embarrass the Saudi government by threatening to exercise their right to breast feed strange men who are willing to drive for them. Goodness knows what will happen when a husband suddenly returns home to find his lactating wife breast feeding a strange man that she is about to employ as a driver!

The BBC has reported (March 5th 2009) that a woman was arrested in Mecca for driving her car. The driving ban on women, moreover, has even been extended to golf carts since I first wrote my book eight years ago. This is a monumental absurdity that is of course infantile and insane and it goes to prove that nothing very much has changed for women's rights – including their right to drive cars – since I wrote my book back in 2003.

But what has changed since the first edition of my book – at least four pioneering chapters of which are devoted to the plight of women in the desert kingdom (notably chapter ten in this book with regard to female employment) – is that Saudi women are beginning to speak out for themselves against the monstrously absurd discrimination that is and has been practised against them. They are also managing to find employment in the workplace more than previously, albeit at a snail's pace and certainly not without almost all workplaces still being segregated single-sex spaces, especially in the public sector.

Whilst many more Saudi women are going to university in the desert kingdom than before, it is estimated that still only about 15% of the labour force is female – a modest change not to be sneezed at in such a traditionally sexist and patriarchal society. Saudi royalty appears to support employment rights for women, but royalty has its die-hard clerics to think about, so it must play its cards carefully, or so we are told (and this is really tough on women!). But there is now one woman in the Saudi government's cabinet, and law and engineering degrees are reportedly available to women these days, as are jobs in business and finance.

So there has been a change here, but not with regard to sexual segregation in most of the workplaces.

The object of bringing these and so many other weird and backward-thinking matters to the attention of the outside world in the pages of this book is, hopefully, to encourage change for the better for the citizens of Saudi Arabia in the not too distant future. The object is not to insult Saudi Arabia, as some reactionaries have claimed. On the contrary, to write about this in the outside world is to be in sympathy with the Saudi people who deserve better – the women who want to drive their cars and not be segregated from men, and the men and women who do not want to stone people to death or behead them for their crimes, or flog them and amputate their hands. To write about these matters is to offer a caring voice of reason to the desert kingdom.

Saudi Arabia's rulers need to lighten up and to get real about so many things that are putting the clock back for their people and making them a laughing stock in the eyes of the world. Time stands still in the desert kingdom, not because time naturally stands still in our lives, but because its rulers are preventing it from moving forward, because they are preventing their people from moving it forward, preventing it in all the backward and primitive ways explained in these pages, which is why virtually nothing has changed since the first edition of this book was published eight years ago.

Because the chapters originally published in my first edition are a history in themselves – the first draft of a history that did not exist previously, the first draft of where Saudi Arabia was and still is coming from in the modern world and a testament to this – they are for all time and can be repeated again without alteration therefore eight years later. As an historical document and framework of fact that is a witness to history, the chapters in this book stand for all time, just as any other history book stands for all time, unless and until things change substantially for the better in the desert kingdom, when a new book can perhaps be written about the nature of those changes. Thankfully, history does not get rewritten to disguise the facts of what went previously, or to excuse what remains of it, as so much of it does still remain in Saudi Arabia today.

In the West there is a tradition of civilising and reforming European literature on such matters, and this is a tradition to which *The Beheading and Other True Stories* belongs. This is a literary tradition that goes back at least as far as 1899 when – 112 years ago – the French journalist, author and playwright, Octave Mirbeau published *The Torture Garden* (1899-1912).

Whilst I have not read *The Torture Garden* and was not aware of it when I first wrote my Saudi book in 2003, I can well understand that Mirbeau wrote his book to make his readers think more carefully and humanely about an historical period in which the pages of their history were written in murder and blood, as were periods in other European nations' histories (so we have all been there, it's not just the Saudis). Mirbeau dedicated his book to the priests, soldiers, judges, educators, instructors and rulers in France whose consciences he wanted to prick and whose policies he wanted to reform, and in due course things changed for the better in France. And that is precisely what I am trying to do in this book about Saudi Arabia 112 years later.

But not since George Orwell's *A Hanging*, eighty years ago in 1931, have we had such a book in the English language as *The Beheading and Other True Stories*, so I guess my book is a milestone in English Literature, and not just a ground-breaking 'first' in terms of including Saudi Arabia in the European tradition of public execution and institutionalised torture literature.

This is a literature that has been pioneered not only in France, but Germany, Czechoslovakia, Austria, Britain and Russia by such notable exponents as Franz Kafka (*In the Penal Colony*, 1914), Vladimir Nabokov (*Invitation to a Beheading*, 1935), and George Orwell (*A Hanging*, 1931). As we see, it is not only Saudi Arabia that has needed to be reformed! But it is chief among the remaining countries that still needs to be reformed, for which judicial and legal reform is woefully long overdue.

My book is the latest in this reforming tradition, eighty long years after Orwell, which is a long space of time, is it not? And given that I had not read Orwell's, Kafka's or Nabokov's books until after I had been to Saudi Arabia and written my own, there is no way in which my book can be described as Orwellian, Kafkaesque or Nabokovian, other than in spirit, of course.

With all this in mind, my original document has now been republished in 2011 without alteration or any updating to its chapters, because there is, alas, virtually nothing for it to be updated for, unless it is to report that, in October 2010 Prince Abdulaziz bin Nasser al Saud was found guilty of having murdered his man servant in the Landmark Hotel in London in a vicious crime with an alleged homosexual element to it.

Not all Saudis or other Muslims agree with what is going on in the desert kingdom today and has been going on there throughout its history. There are those who deplore it.

Since I first wrote this book, I have had some good fan mail, and paid careful attention to it (woe betide the author who neglects what his readers are saying!). What interests me is how different readers read things, not only differently, but also the same! It is particularly pleasing to me that some have been subtle enough to pick up on the humanitarian nature of my book, rather than the grisly and distressing shock-horror, both of which are in these pages in equal measure. Grisly shock-horror on its own is hardly worth writing or reading and may even be gratuitous. It is what one can intelligently make of the shock-horror that makes the difference. For example, former *Sunday Times* journalist and Cambridge natural sciences graduate, James Poole, now in retirement, has emailed as follows: 'What you say is absolutely spot on. What is it journalists are supposed to do if not hold a light up to power? And you are so true in the way you describe the diplomatic covering up and lies that are 'not useful' to the diplomats' current political masters. It is interesting to me that you fundamentally do not approach your task through an economic prism. It's my background in business journalism, of course, but I almost always look for what is interesting in the economic relationships. You are much more focused on the people and not the fat cats. Yours is a humanitarian book – a claim which you make and can be proud of.'

A City of London banker and St Andrew's University modern languages graduate, Alex Jablonowksi, emails to say: 'I really liked it. It almost stands alone as a serious piece of journalism, gently drawing out the paradoxes. A lovely piece of writing.'

Because so many people only ever think of Saudi Arabia as an oil rich politico-economic power – that it's best not to upset! – or a vast and empty desert, the ordinary Saudi people and the precise detail of so many of the ugly/sinister aspects of their ruthless, inhumane and oppressive treatment, gets conveniently overlooked, unless and until it is spelt out in a book of this kind, and for the first time in Saudi Arabian history, which brings us back to my claim at the beginning of this introduction that this book is a pioneering document and testament to history that has not been published previously and will presumably stand for all time therefore.

I make this claim modestly, but pointedly, because it is too easily overlooked in the politico-economic climate that generally dominates our thinking about the desert kingdom, suggesting that the humanitarian considerations are, at best, a secondary consideration, or at worst, of no consequence whatsoever!

Bob Crew
London, January 2011

PREFACE

In the 1970s, there was a famous little column in the satirical magazine *Private Eye* called 'Under the Wilton', regarded as infamous by many in diplomatic and other quarters in the desert kingdom of Saudi Arabia where I was *The Times* correspondent.

Much of this column was written by me from the seaport city of Jeddah, sometimes smuggling my copy out in a friendly diplomatic bag (yes, there are such things), other times relying on colleagues to post it for me from Heathrow Airport, when they were flying back to the UK, in order to avoid the risk of my mail being tampered with by Saudi Arabian postal workers. They were instructed to open envelopes randomly, en route to the outside world, so that the authorities could take a quick look at the contents to decide whether they approved or not.

There were plenty of unpleasant aspects to the desert

kingdom that were being swept under the carpet at that time – aspects that are still being swept under the carpet today – and the *Private Eye* column was named after Sir John Wilton, the British Ambassador in Jeddah, who was not short of such things under his carpet, of course. Since I spoke with Sir John and Lady Wilton on a regular basis, and had numerous contacts inside the British and other foreign embassies, I was in an excellent position to write the *Eye*'s column which, as I recall, was edited in its Soho offices by Paul Foot, and the then editor Richard Ingrams, although it is possible that the late Auberon Waugh had a hand in it, too. This was before anyone had heard of the media bunny Ian Hislop – the current editor of the *Eye*.

Because there were things about Saudi Arabia that were being covered up in those days, things that continue to be covered up today, we are reminded that, whilst everything changes in theory, in practice nothing changes very much or at all. Such unchanged things that were satirised in 'Under the Wilton' included Saudi Arabia's extremist medieval mindset, its ancient customs and laws, its outrageous prejudices and its attitude to women and the outside world, all of which continue to be swept under a carpet even more massive and lumpy than before.

For this reason, the true and/or true-to-life short stories, tales and eyewitness accounts in the following pages of this book are entirely valid as we embark on the twenty-first century, dealing as they do with things that are kept under wraps or not generally spoken about or analysed in the necessary detail, and not least because there is renewed concern currently about the position of Saudi Arabia in our deeply troubled world. From a Western and democratic perspective, understanding what makes the desert kingdom tick is by no means easy – it is not easy from any modern perspective anywhere in the world – and, when confronted by a strange and alien medieval system, it is hard to comprehend how the better-educated Saudis can possibly tolerate and endorse such a system. Some people in the West and elsewhere say that it is not right to judge others, but I do not agree with this. The Saudis are into judgement big time. They judge the women they stone to death and the people whom they execute and flog in public. They also judge the outside world from their own narrow and bigoted point of view. So we should not delude ourselves that we – or the United Nations for that matter – have no right to judge them by our standards. We do. Judgement Day for Saudi Arabia is long overdue (as, no doubt, it is for us all).

Because the darker side of life in the desert kingdom overshadows everything else, only an ostrich with its head deep in the desert sand could possibly ignore this, so I make no apology for dwelling on its lurid and inescapably grisly detail with a clinical and hopefully pedantic eye. Most of these stories do not make for comfortable reading (anyone seriously and honestly interested in Saudi Arabia does not expect or deserve comfortable reading). Some of these stories are 100 per cent factual, whilst others are honestly told apocryphal and 'factional' stories that turn journalism and other information into literature. What they have in common is that they are all true and that they have been stored up and committed to memory for long enough for them to ripen and mature.

Characters in the fictional/factional stories are not necessarily to be confused with real-life people or events and any resemblance to any living person is purely coincidental. It has been necessary to invent such characters to disguise the identity and change the names of some people, in order to protect the innocent and, in those cases, any comparison with others who may mistakenly believe that they are wrongly identified should be firmly resisted. It has also been necessary to be occasionally elliptical, but only occasionally.

There is unofficial leaked information, official information, reported information and my own personal experiences and observations, all carefully drawn and blended together here in a sincere portrait of life to provide readers with – as Oscar Wilde said of Kipling's *Plain Tales from the Hills* in 1890 – the feeling that 'one were seated under a palm tree reading life ... he terrifies us with his truth', a feeling of what Kipling himself described as 'heat and bewilderment and wasted effort' in those far-off days.

Terrifying people with the – or one's – truth is still the name of the game. It was forever thus, and there is still heat, bewilderment and wasted effort, including many terrifying truths, in this wicked world, as we put distance between ourselves and Kipling – truly horrible truths that need to be carefully examined and courageously told. So seekers after truth should be prepared to be terrified. These are fiercely thought-provoking stories, some of which are vicious, and they are not for those who cannot bear looking at things as they are. But neither are they purely voyeuristic. I have endowed them, I hope, with sufficient psychological insight, moral concern and empathy to make them so much more than gratuitous voyeurism. Even so, they are a bitter pill to swallow, and readers may find that they need a cast-iron constitution.

Any decent writer must fearlessly pursue his or her own understanding of a place, regardless of the outcome, telling the brutal truth about it as he or she sees it, however devastating or disagreeable that may be, however unflattering or critical it may be. Writers must find their own way into the truth without regard to the consequences. That's what good writers do. They cannot help themselves. If a writer's view of a place is relentlessly negative, it's no good resenting this and complaining that he has presented only half the picture. What's the point of complaining that there is more to the place in question than he has allowed for? This may or may not be true, but this is beside the point – the half-picture on which he has fixed is the point that should concern readers. The thing to do is to ask whether the half that is presented – or two-thirds in the case of Saudi Arabia – is sufficient in itself to justify the picture on offer. It is not a writer's job to emphasise positives at the expense of the sinister negatives that overshadow them, especially when there have already been plenty of books that romance the legendary mystique of the desert and glamorise the fabulous wealth of today's oil sheikhs. What is required is the bold hand of the artist to lay bare the horrid facts.

And readers should resist shooting the messenger.

The thing to do is to think about that message and its method of delivery and ask yourself if it increases your knowledge and expands your consciousness. If a book's message does this, then there can surely be no doubt that it is literature of a necessary and perhaps worthy kind. If it does not, then chuck the book away.

The first of the stories in the following pages – which is the central story in the collection – is *The Beheading*, an account of a man being beheaded in a public place in Saudi Arabia.

The chances are that not since George Orwell wrote his short story, *A Hanging*, in 1931 – and Kafka wrote *In the Penal Colony* in the 1920s – has there been such an explicit and focused story about an execution, conveying the full horror and inhumanity of such a barbaric and brutal punishment as a man having his head severed from his body in the queasy name of justice.

Again, the reader is warned that, because this is a very analytical and soul-searching story, sincerely told by a storyteller who has suffered for his subject, he or she had better be prepared to suffer likewise. I am a writer who wants to share all the pain with readers, without sparing them anything.

Whilst some of the stories in this collection are dark and unsettling, others are intended to be witty and satirical. But they are all told from the heart – I seldom, if ever, do things half-heartedly – and with such authority as any journalist or short-story writer can be expected to have because he knows his subject, having been to where he has been, and seen what he's seen.

I am glad to say that none of these stories are politically correct, and I think it is worth mentioning this because English literature on the subject of Arabia and the Arabs has, in my view, been far too politically correct previously, woefully pretending that Bedouin and other Arabs are more noble and gentlemanly than they are, romanticising them out of all reality and proportion, whilst turning a massive blind eye to the sickening and outrageous detail of their darker side.

In particular, I am thinking of travel books, romanticised narratives of war and adventure, and personal and imperial diaries from such legendary 'great thinkers' on this subject as Gertrude Bell, Thesiger, Philby, T.E. Lawrence and others, the latter of whom wrote *Seven Pillars of Wisdom*, rich in Oxfordisms and mythology, was hailed as a great work of scholarly literature (which it probably is), even though it got the Arabs completely wrong and told us much more about T.E. Lawrence and his brand of literature than it did about the Arabs. Only a scholar – and an apologist White Arab – could achieve such a thing! *Seven Pillars of Wisdom* was printed as a private limited edition in 1926 when a private sector of British society thought that it alone had the copyright on the way in which the Arabs were perceived in the UK.

I realise that, to express these views, is heresy, and I shall no doubt have the literary world come down on me like a ton of bricks as a result, but I'm sticking to my guns and my argument just the same. And I'm sticking to the traditions of Kipling, Kafka and Orwell, whom I regard as far better writers and 'thinkers' than these British White Arabs (about whom there is a story in this collection). This book does not claim to be a scholarly work or even a recent history (unless, of course, we can agree that journalism is always the first draft of history). It merely claims to be a collection of highly personal and personalised short stories – some factual and others fictional or factional (the distinguishing marks of which are intended to be self-evident) – that readers will either like or not.

These are stories that have haunted my imagination in such a way as to help me recreate, in what aims to be a vivid and meaningful fashion, some of the major miseries and complicated mysteries of the darker side of life in the desert kingdom today. In the telling of some stories I have provided a discourse – in the form of background commentaries and/or dialogue between characters – on how such stories should or should not be told (how they are constructed and written) and this, too, may add to their interest.

The fact that they are written more than a quarter of a century after I was in permanent residence in the desert kingdom is neither here nor there. Kipling wrote *Kim* 13 years after he left India and this brilliant novel was no less relevant for that. And, as it happens, I have returned to the kingdom since I first lived there and have kept up with events more recently, so I have been able to update many of the stories as appropriate.

Whilst some of these stories may be rubbished by a goodly number of highly defensive Saudi Arabians and their chums, who would rather not see them in print, I do know that they will be welcomed by others. Some stories may also be rubbished by the politically correct among us, who seem to think that we should not be criticising Muslims in any shape or form, for fear of tarring them all with the same brush – what an absurd idea! But to them I would simply say that this is not a criticism of all Muslims, or Arabians for that matter, so kindly pipe down.

If these stories are a criticism at all, they are criticising not more than a relative handful of Saudi Arabian rulers who are out of step with the morality and humanity of the rest of the world and want to keep the desert kingdom that way. Neither are my stories 'anti-Saudi Arabian', as is clear from *The Silly Goose And Its Golden Egg* and *All Hail to the House of Saud*.

But to quote the investigative journalist John Pilger – whom I have not met since my Hong Kong days when I spent an evening with him and his former wife, Scarf Flett, in a London wine bar on return from the former Crown Colony – Saudi Arabia is 'the most extreme Islamic regime on earth, where apostates are beheaded. Women have no rights; it is illegal for a woman even to drive a car.' This view was published in the 27 May 2002 edition of the *Daily Mirror*, and if any regime deserves criticism, this one certainly does.

John Pilger also reminds us that, while many female public figures have 'denounced the "brutal oppression of women" in Afghanistan by the Taliban and demanded their emancipation', they have 'remained silent on the medieval treatment of Saudi women in the spiritual home of Al-Qaeda' for the obvious reason that 'Saudi Arabia has most of the world's oil'.

And there's the rub. They have the oil. But perhaps the rest of us can appeal to their conscience some time soon. And perhaps we can stand up to them for a change. When, in recent years, ITV produced *Death of a Princess*, and the Saudi Arabian Government caused one hell of a stink about this in diplomatic and political circles in London, someone in the British Government asked for the material to be destroyed (so that the programme could not be repeated again, presumably). And it has indeed been destroyed, according to an email in my possession from Carlton Television archives confirming this. Clearly, there is a need to stand up to our friends and allies in this world, as well as our enemies, and we should let them know that it is in their own best interests that we do so. If the House of Saud wishes to survive forever – and there is no guarantee that it will – it should perhaps lighten up a little and listen to its friends.

When one goes to Saudi Arabia, one cannot help but look into the heart of darkness, if one is sharp-eyed. And if an author is to write truthfully about the desert kingdom, he has no choice but to accept a poisoned chalice. Of course, Saudi Arabia is a great place for an investigative journalist from Britain, because there is so much more to investigate than at home in the UK. It's a great place for a journalist to make a name for himself. In a closed and unjust society, in which a veil is pulled in more ways than one over so many things – in which a blind eye is turned to so many wrongs that are locked away beyond the public view – one cannot fail to investigate even the most commonplace things. For this reason, the *Saudi Gazette* English-language newspaper in Jeddah, of which I was a founding member, was removed from the newsstands and closed down on more than one occasion during its infancy. These days, the newspaper has, alas, been well and truly tamed by the Government, so it can be relied upon to censor itself and not make waves, as a result of which the few investigative journalists that it had – not least the incomparable Jack Lundin, currently in South Africa – are long gone. When I was not corresponding for *The Times* in Saudi Arabia, I was producing two pages daily for the *Saudi Gazette*.

During my time in Saudi Arabia, I lived in Jeddah, but travelled widely, visiting and working in such places as Riyadh, Dhahran, Yenbow, Jubail, Taif and Abia Ali, to mention but a few. I came to know the country like the back of my hand and I inadvertently became a Muslim because the Saudi Embassy in Cairo mistakenly wrote Muslim into my passport when I handed it in there, so that my application for a work permit could be processed, before returning ten days later to collect it. I expect it was because the permit was scrawled in Arabic that I failed to notice that the Saudis had got my religion wrong, but when I returned to Jeddah, a Saudi friend pointed out that I had become a Muslim, courtesy of the Saudi Arabian Embassy! But he cautioned against my going to Mecca, even though my passport would have got me into the holy city ... although I am not sure that I would have got out again. Since I was obliged to have a statement of the Christian religion stapled into my British passport in order to get into the desert kingdom in the first place – the Saudis were determined to keep Jews out of the 'land of the pure', as they call it – it is odd, to say the least, that the Saudi Embassy in Cairo should have made such a mistake. I had graduated from being a Christian to a Muslim in a matter of months. It now only remains for me to become a Jew and a Hindu as well, in order to qualify for a place in heaven on account of any of these religions.

A sense of humour comes in handy in Saudi Arabia where there is much to try one's patience and to trouble the conscience when exposed to the darker side of life.

When telling gruelling stories of this sort, a writer needs to have an awareness of the right kind of style or rhetoric, not only for the occasion, but also for his readers, so there is always the 'intolerable wrestle with words and meanings' to which T S Eliot referred in 1940 (times and writing styles may change, but the literary problem remains the same). Do we fit the writer to his readers, or do we give them something entirely different for a change? Do we tell the story precisely as it is, however macabre or ugly – and, if so, will readers have the stomach for it? Or do we also tell it how it *feels* to the writer and appeals to his imagination, in which case, can the writer succeed in taking his readers with him into his own consciousness (adverse criticism he may be able to live with, but he cannot live without his readers)? The golden rule of effective creative writing and story-telling for me – and I hope that it shows in this collection – is always to go directly to the heart of the matter and tell it clearly and explicitly, not only how it is, but also how it feels, and tell it, furthermore, with as much *enthusiasm* and/or *imagination* for the subject as one can muster. But telling a story how it feels is risky because, as everybody knows there are profound differences in personal taste and preferred styles among readers when writing becomes subjective. Even so, it is not for a creative writer to chicken out of this on that account. He must deal with the emotional side of the stories that he has walked into, and he must remain true to his feelings and his chosen style, without sacrificing the facts of the matter. Of course, many of the ghastly and depressing factual stories in the following pages are calculated to kill enthusiasm stone dead, but it is important to remember that it is enthusiasm for the precious truth about the mind-blowing incomprehensibility of the matter that counts here, not enthusiasm for the gory nature and morbid details of the stories themselves. What matters most is enthusiasm for the truthful and imaginative telling of stories that need to be told.

Unless one is thrown into a rat-infested Saudi jail – crawling with cockroaches and echoing with the shrieks of unbridled torture – it is not exactly Conrad's permanent 24-hour-a-day darkness that is being experienced, but it is darkness once or twice a week or a fortnight, which is more than enough for most of us. And it is this occasional and menacing darkness – in contrast to the endless rounds of bright and breezy business receptions, glittering state visits, and poolside barbecue parties in rich people's gardens – with which this collection is concerned. So the fact that we are about to step into a minefield in this collection is utterly predictable.

1

THE BEHEADING

One day I ask myself, 'Why don't I go to a beheading?' I suppose that I have to witness one before leaving this wretched country and returning to London. As an investigative journalist, I should not turn a blind eye to the darker side of life in this or any other part of the world, and I do have a duty to witness history and to see what lessons can be learned from it. No point in shrinking from the ugly fact that convicted rapists and murderers are being publicly beheaded every week here, while I and others sleep soundly in our beds, and with a clear conscience. No point in ignoring the distressing and deeply repugnant reality that adulterous women are being stoned to death. Then there are the thieves having their hands chopped off. If people have to endure these barbaric and inhumane acts, the least that any sincere and serious writer can do is witness them in order to convey to others their full horror and obscenity.

Having chickened out of such grisly matters during my first six months in the desert kingdom, it's time that I take a deep breath and get them over and done with. It's certainly not morbid curiosity on my part ... is it? No, I don't think so. It is, rather, a compassionate compulsion to get at the ugly truth and expose it. To shake it by the throat, however disgusting and revolting it may be, and to face the unpleasant facts of life in this part of the world.

I am in the desert kingdom of Saudi Arabia where I am employed as *The Times* correspondent, interviewing Saudi government ministers, foreign diplomats, politicians and businessmen about the kingdom's fabulous oil wealth and its trade relations with the outside world. The outside world is the far side of the moon compared to this place. It is light years and centuries ahead of this medieval desert kingdom to which I can only have been sent, for my sins, as some sort of punishment posting! I must have done something very wicked to have finished up here.

I am writing about investment prospects in this part of the world and the politico-economic situation to which its huge reserves of oil have given rise. I am carrying a certificate of the Christian religion in my passport and I also have a 'to whom it may concern' letter from Rodney Cowton at *The Times*, in the hope that this will win friends and influence people for me, by opening doors in a closed community that is generally suspicious of foreigners and traditionally unaccustomed to Western journalists on its shores (and increasingly alarmed by the fact that more of them are arriving by the day).

It is the first time that anyone can remember that *The Times* has had a correspondent permanently based in this erstwhile forbidden outpost. Previously, Robert Fisk covered it from a distance in Cairo. It is also the first time that the local English-language *Saudi Gazette* newspaper has had a business editor (another of my responsibilities).

And it is to be the first and last time that I shall see a public beheading with my own eyes and write about it.

Not that I have to go very far to see one, because the hotel in which I am staying – the Omar Khyam in downtown Jeddah, next-door to the *souk* – is adjacent to the square in which there are usually beheadings every Friday. I have been in the hotel for six months while heads have rolled outside, without giving them a second thought, because to give them a second thought would, of course, drive me in the direction of this Saudi Arabian blood sport, about which I have not yet been prepared to write. But now I am as ready as I shall ever be, so I am determined to do the ghastly deed.

A Saudi Arabian colleague says to me, 'There will be another beheading this week. Black Abdullah is coming to town to execute somebody or other, who richly deserves to have his head chopped off, according to popular opinion.'

I enquire, 'What crime has he committed?'

'Who knows? Who cares? Most people take the jaundiced view that the filthy man must have done something perfectly dreadful if he is going to be beheaded. Rape or murder – one of the two – both are unacceptable in this country, where we do not pussyfoot around with such criminals, as you do in Britain. There hasn't been much about it in the papers, naturally, just a short, tight-lipped announcement declaring the criminal's guilt. The usual thing. But why don't you go and see it? Everybody says that Abdullah is a master craftsman and I think it must be so, because a friend of mine once saw him at work with his cutlass, and tells me that he is absolutely superb – a real perfectionist, so masterful and precise. It puts my teeth on edge and sends shivers down my spine just to talk about it.'

My colleague laughs out loud. He has a fine sense of sarcasm, sharp as a razor. He is one of life's piss-takers, always ready to wind people and life up for his own amusement ... I like his style. He has forgotten to mention habitual stealing. One can be beheaded for that as well, but no matter.

'Rumour has it that once you've seen Black Abdullah doing his thing with a man's head,' he drools theatrically, 'you'll never want to watch anybody else. Since you are always complaining of boredom in this country and how fed up you are, perhaps it will give you a lift to go and watch a beheading. Perhaps you should make it your business to watch one every week, as so many people do in this windswept city of ours. It might give you something to look forward to.'

'Very funny,' I reply, 'you have *such* a dark and bitter-sweet sense of humour.'

'In this country, it's a tool of survival, wouldn't you say? How else can we live with ourselves?'

A 'lift' is exactly what I need, although I do not expect for one moment that I shall get such an improbable thing from watching a beheading, which sounds like a real downer. But I am soon to learn that a 'lift' is what beheadings give most of the Arabian masses that regularly turn out to watch them in the drab desert kingdom, where time crawls as slowly as a snail, and hardly anything ever happens most days of the week in this go-nowhere, do-nothing, overheated country. It is a place where virtually nothing happens, not once or twice, but so many times.

While my Arabian colleague, who is in his late thirties, tells me that he has seen plenty of beheadings over the years – since

26

he was a young boy – he regrets that he has never seen the celebrated Black Abdullah doing his thing with his cutlass, although he has always dreamed of having the good fortune to do so one of these days. Young and old Arabians follow different executioners, just as their counterparts in the Western world follow champion boxers, footballers and pop stars. Executioners are their heroes and sometimes even their role models – the Mohammed Alis and Mike Tysons of the desert kingdom. Oh yes! A beheading by Abdullah is just what the doctor ordered for a crestfallen younger man who is bored out of his skull. What a splendid idea!

My colleague says, 'Would you like me to use my influence to get you a balcony seat in one of the houses around the square where the beheading is to take place? People are paying a high price for overhanging balconies, but one of my friends may be able to smuggle you in free of charge.'

'No thanks. I think I shall prefer to stand in the crowd, so that I can slip away without notice if I suddenly decide that enough is enough. I may need to go off for a quick vomit.'

'Oh, surely not? I thought you English were made of sterner stuff. But one certainly gets the atmosphere so much better in the crowd, standing shoulder to shoulder with everybody else. It is so much more exciting and one is not as coolly detached as those up in the balconies who view it from a respectable distance. Also, with so many high-born women allowed on to the balconies on these occasions, where they are free to remove their veils for once, in order to have a clear view, there is always the complicated problem of which balcony to choose for the men, who must always be segregated and distanced from the women, of course, otherwise they will be gazing at the women's nakedly revealing faces and making eyes at them, instead of

27

enjoying the spectacle of justice being done at 120 degrees in the shade. We can't have white skins like you distracted by our gorgeous women and gazing into their eyes – full of sexually inviting Eastern promise!'

My colleague – who must remain nameless because he still resides in Saudi Arabia – really does have a fine wit and dry sense of humour.

He is good at sending himself and his people up – foreigners, too – and he is seldom unaware of life's little ironies. So he is excellent company. But he is wrong about justice being done at 120 degrees in the shade. Shade? What shade? In the square where the head will roll, there is no shade. It is the onlookers around the square who will have the benefit of shade in this ferociously hot country, but the poor wretch who will lose his head will lose it under a scorching and angry sun. If the executioner doesn't chop his head off fast, the condemned man will probably die of sunstroke! Waiting for death at more than 120 degrees in the sun – waiting for the sunstroke express for a quick exit to heaven or hell – is no ordinary kind of waiting.

When it comes to beheadings and/or the daily routine of life – and beheadings are certainly routine – one cannot fail to think about the monstrous sun here. It is everywhere, right round the clock, and like a neighbour from hell it gives one no rest, no peace and quiet. It is impossible to get away from it, or to be rid of it, and it is one of the most important things to be understood about this country. The sun is not at all the same sun that is known and understood in Europe and the West. It shadows one's every move, like an ominous and old-familiar stalker. Most people think of the sun as a healthy life-giving force. But in the desert kingdom it is life-threatening and fiendish, as it scorches your soul and devastates all before it, so that next to nothing grows, and the very air itself cannot easily be breathed, on account of its being overheated and dried up, or so it seems, thanks to the tireless and oh-so-tiring sun, so unforgiving, blistering and treacherous, so lethal and dangerous. The sun here is the devil incarnate – a relentless yellow and golden devil. Hardly any grass grows, which is why plastic grass is imported, and hardly anything survives without protection under the great flame-thrower up there in the sky. This is a remorseless sun that does not look kindly upon its people, and protection from it is the name of the game in its merciless, blinding and angry glare, at the hot end of which there is an absence of birdsong in the few trees and parks that survive here. If looks could kill, people would drop dead on the pavements under the fierce glare of the sun.

For every 100 kilometres that one drives in such a sun, the rubber tyres of cars and lorries burst in the excruciating heat, so that it becomes necessary for motorists to take plenty of spares with them on long journeys. Drivers fall asleep behind the wheels of their road vehicles in the too hot desert sun, and so crash into each other, while others see double when the reflection of sun on sand creates a mirage which perilously suggests that drivers are either too near to, or too far from, oncoming vehicles. So they swerve dangerously in this direction or that. It is hardly surprising that desert motorways are littered with crashed vehicles and dead camels that have strayed into their path, as the sun plays havoc with people's lives.

In classical mythology, the sun is reckoned to be the attribute of truth personified, and this is because all is supposed to be revealed by gentle and enlightening sunlight that dispels obscurity, clarifying all before it and defeating darkness with a clear and true vision. But this welcome symbolism does not hold good in the desert kingdom where the devious sun is quick to put out your eyes and destroy your sight, revealing nothing other than a fiery desert cauldron in which there is nothing to be seen or revealed in the bright and golden darkness other than emptiness, or village and town folk taking to their beds every afternoon to avoid the heat, or perhaps dying of thirst when stranded without water in remote parts of the desert. Whilst, in kinder climates, the sun may have revealed the love affair between Mars and Venus, in the land of the pure where Saudi Arabians are reared, this impure sun reveals only its hate and disapproval of every living thing that perishes in its hostile glare.

On the day of the beheading, I am shaded from the sun, as I look out into the sun-drenched, soon to be blood-drenched, square adjacent to Jeddah's Omar Khyam Hotel, where a crowd has gathered to see a man's head fall. I am waiting patiently for the condemned man to arrive, listening to the excited banter and chatter of people gossiping around me.

A hush suddenly falls on the crowd in which I have managed to jostle myself into position in the front row, having arrived in good time. There is no going back now. Too many people are packed in behind me.

This is no ordinary hush. It has fallen like an exploded bomb of monumental silence that is soon to be disturbed by a fleet of noisy police patrol cars and motorcycles (American imports) as it swiftly enters the square in which this beheading is to take place. With their sirens blaring, lights flashing and tyres screeching to a halt, this pack of police cars – snarling like motorised mad dogs – is all part of the carefully stage-managed high drama in the late-morning glare for hundreds of spectators, rapt in morbid fascination, as they gather in the square to enjoy a good beheading. Many will have stopped en route to their place of worship in the mosque, where they are due to offer up their prayers to Allah.

After the police cars and motorcycles have positioned themselves in the four corners of this crowded square, with their engines finally turned off, there is silence again, silence everywhere, as the expectant crowd holds its breath in the stifling heat, waiting for an ambulance to arrive without delay, as I hear that it always does, hot on the heels of the police, and followed by yet another police patrol car.

As the last police car follows a solitary and unremarkable ambulance into the square through a cloud of dust, full of gritty foreboding, and grinds to a ceremonious halt, the operatic scene is complete.

Two armed policemen step out from the back of one of the cars with their criminal victim, and they escort him to a central position, where he is to lose his precious head, before beady and gleeful eyes under fevered brows, looking out at him from the surrounding shade, glowing like burnt embers in a shadowy fire. Some people's eyes are bursting with excited anticipation, popping out of their heads as if on adrenalin stalks. Others are set deep, smouldering and glaring.

Forcing their victim – who does not struggle as he goes meekly to his fate – on to his knees, the policemen tie his hands behind his back and then blindfold him. Had he been someone whose identity the police wished to conceal from the outset, for reasons best known to themselves, I am told that he would have appeared hooded.

As they do this, the executioner suddenly emerges from the

back seat of another police car and strides purposefully towards his prey, with his magnificent shiny cutlass in hand, glistening and shimmering in the hot sun, giving off cool reflections like golden butterflies flitting overhead.

A tall black man with king-size biceps, the executioner is powerfully built, with overdeveloped muscles shining in his own bright sweat as it trickles down his highly polished, ebony-black skin. He holds his head high and his back erect, straight as an arrow. It is Black Abdullah, as my colleague has foretold, and he is, by all accounts, known throughout the desert kingdom as the best executioner in the land, capable of slicing a man's head clean off his neck in one super clean sweep of his feared and revered cutlass, striking the neck precisely at the right angle – striking in the name of God – in order that the head will fall precisely where it is intended to fall, on a spotless lily-white towel, placed several feet ahead of the victim's bowed head.

My Arabian colleague has explained this to me in advance and there are American, British and European spectators in the crowd, excitedly chattering about this. I hear a Brit say, 'We ought to have this in the UK. If somebody raped my wife, I would want his head for it. As for my wife, she would probably want his balls!'

To sever a head with a single strike, instead of having to hack at the unyielding neck several times in order to do the trick, and to aim that head in the direction of the clean white towel, patiently awaiting its prey, rather than overshooting or undershooting the towel and falling beyond or before it in the sand, is the name of the game, the executioner's game. It is, by all accounts, quite an art, and only the celebrated few can do it. Some make a ghastly mess of it, too horrible to behold, as they hack away at a stubborn head that refuses to budge and to be separated from its neck. Others come close to getting it right, but never quite manage to perfect their art. It is said that this head has to be struck at the right angle if it is not to roll down the victim's chest and land in his lap. But Black Abdullah has not been known to fail, because he is a great perfectionist who has studied and thought much about these macabre matters, and when people hear that he is coming to their town or village to do the business, they praise the lord and turn out from far and wide to see him. They turn out to admire his skill and to feast their eyes on his muscular body, as he does his thing with the severed head of a worthless criminal.

I notice a young Arabian man in the crowd with big and beautiful brown eyes – soft, gentle and fluid like a woman's – and they are riveted, morbidly drinking in all this blinding obscenity and reflecting it, keen not to miss out on any of the gory details, which are mirrored in his eyes as surely as they are imprinted on his immature young soul. The human eye, like the hand, is supposed to be the tool and symbol of God the Father, since it is all-seeing and affords God's people the precious gift of sight with which to see the way ahead and to distinguish between good and bad, ugliness and beauty, in this wicked world. But what a thing to do with such a precious gift on this gruesome occasion, what an ugly sight to behold, what an abuse of sight and a beautiful pair of eyes, what a shocking reminder that, if you live with your head down a drain, your beautiful eyes are of little use. Even as lanterns in this bright darkness, there is little of beauty or goodness for the eyes to see.

But in the cheerful un-severed heads and gleeful eyes of the regulars in this crowd – yes, they are regulars, according to my

Arabian colleague who has suddenly turned up to tap me on the shoulder and point them out to me – it is the evil eye that is at work here. They are protruding eyes, bursting their blood vessels; fanatically judgemental and bloodthirsty eyes that would, no doubt, love to see the eyes of others put out, out of their skulls. They are deranged, psychopathic eyes, many of them, to remind us that in the land of the blind, the one-eyed man is inevitably and all-powerfully king; of course he is.

After the executioner has sliced off his victim's head and landed it on target, without mishap, he is expected to do one of two things, according to my Arabian colleague. If the victim is particularly notorious and wildly hated, it is rumoured that the executioner may sometimes hook the head on the tip of his cutlass and hold it high in the air for all to see, smiling and proudly beaming his satisfaction at the spectators, who may very well applaud and cheer by return, as the proud swordsman marches round the square, displaying the severed head, just as the triumphant captain of a football team in Britain holds up a silver cup to an admiring crowd after his team have won a tournament.

But if the victim is a nobody, who is only averagely hated for his improperly tried crimes, then a medic from the back of the ambulance simply takes the four corners of the towel and ties them in a pretty little bow at the centre, over the top of his severed head, before carrying this blood-stained parcel off and putting it in the back of the ambulance, while policemen scoop up the decapitated body and put that in the back of the ambulance as well.

And this is what happens on this occasion after a wave of loud gasps from different sections of the crowd – as the head is lifted from its neck and flung through the air – and after there have been some stifled moans and groans at the revolting sight of a severed head being swatted like a fly by a highly polished cutlass.

It suddenly dawns on me how quickly and carelessly our precious lives can so fatally turn to grim death, almost without giving the matter a second heart-breaking thought in the unfeeling minds of some people. This man's head that I have seen so savagely severed from its living body, gliding through the air like a blood-smeared dart in the direction of a lily-white towel, before falling with a thud, dead as a stone, was a *live head* on which his wavy black hair was still growing and shining when the death blow fell only minutes earlier! The hair in his eyebrows was still growing as his body sweat streamed salt through his blindfold and into his eyes, and soaking his shirt and underclothes. All of his control mechanisms for his conscious and unconscious functions – such as breathing and digestion – were functioning according to plan. No doubt he was breathing more heavily and perhaps having a serious panic attack, but he was still breathing. The nerves by which we register sensations, such as pain and temperature, were functioning according to plan before they were ruthlessly severed by the executioner's cutlass, which cut through his neck and prevented his oxygenated blood-flow to his brain. If this man's head had not been severed inside two fleeting minutes – the mercurial time that it takes for the brain to be damaged when it is short of blood – he would have died of brain damage as well! Protected by the bones of his skull, this man's brain and its nerve pathways – with all the infinite and magical interconnections that determine his intelligence and creativity – must surely have become gridlocked when his neck met with the sharp edge of the cutlass and his head suffered a massive trauma in consequence. All of his sinuses, glands and senses must surely have blown a fuse in the final blackout of his mind.

His was a live head in which, presumably, panic-stricken thoughts were still being created right up to the last, while life and/or death was quite possibly being imagined behind his blindfolded eyes and tightly clenched teeth.

There is an inescapable emotional and moral attitude to these vile executions which are not new to literature – both Dickens and Kafka have described hangings in their work – as George Orwell observed, back in 1931, when he wrote his exceedingly short story, *The Hanging*, about an Indian convict being hanged by the British in the days of Empire. Orwell it was who emphasised the stark difference between a live and a dead head, in order to get his message over that life is both precious and sacred.

The head that I have seen so cruelly severed from its neck, with the blood spurting out of it, was a head in which, moments previously, the refreshing blood of life was still rushing to a brain that was still sending out its signals to the rest of the body, whilst nerves were still being nervy, before they were suddenly cut short. Perhaps the man being topped was so overwhelmed by hideous and ghastly fear and dire apprehension that he was pissing himself in his underpants, because his was a *living and precious head* that was about to be severed, not some dead and dopey lump of meat, or poisonous growth that needed to be surgically removed. It had a brain with memory cells that had not forgotten how to remember – God knows what they could have been remembering at the point of death – and it had a porous skin that still knew how to sweat, as well as eyes that could still perceive beauty and shed tears, ears that responded to sweet music, a fevered brow that had not, as yet, lost the habit of frowning, a nose that knew how to sniff and to smell, teeth that could chatter in the cold, a mouth that could salivate because it still had the use of its glands, a tongue that could taste and lips that could smile and kiss.

The head that I have just seen cut from its neck, with its own precious mind and intellect still intact, had been *fully alive and conscious* when it was ruthlessly cut off in a despicable public place, before the prying and curious eyes – and indifferent stony hearts – of those whose consciousness of what it means to cheapen and savagely destroy life in this way seems to be remarkably limited in the extreme, as they turn their backs on a headless body and calmly walk away from the scene of the crime, many of them looking forward to the next time ... and the next ... and the next ...

Having been severed while it was still functioning, with all its faculties neatly in place, this head was still distinguishing itself from all that is lifeless, *because it was so very much alive*. Who knows or cares or can possibly imagine what this head could have been thinking and feeling at the point of death? Who knows whether its blindfolded eyes were incurious both to life and the head's approaching fate in the form of the executioner's cutlass, out of sight but hardly out of mind?

When a condemned man's blood has been spilled under the sharp cutting edge of the executioner's sword, it is the preciousness of life itself that is being spilled likewise, and it is humanity and the humane life that is being ripped apart. A decapitated body and a lifeless severed head are all that are left – two bizarre and inanimate objects that have lost their charm, have lost the magical power of precious life.

But to whom is life precious on this occasion? To whom was the condemned man's life precious? Not to most people in this crowd, that's for sure, but to the severed head's owner certainly, and to his family, friends and loved ones, hopefully. Yet his head has been snapped off, just like that, as if it were the detachable head of a plastic doll, the leaden head of a toy soldier – as if it were the worthless head of a rag doll that could be cut off, just like that. And it has become a revolting and sickening sight, this gory severed head that no longer belongs to its body.

Having turned out to witness this cruel and barbaric spectacle, I must now convey it in a form of words that do not shrink from unpleasant facts, or dwell too perversely upon them either. But there must be no shielding people from the gruesome detail of ugly truth, or from brutal and inhumane reality, if I am to convey the full horror of what has happened here today. I must see if I can capture the atmosphere and the *feeling* of the ugly facts of this horrific event. I need to discover how best to say something like 'yes, this is what happened, but more importantly this is also how it felt, this is a *felt experience* that I am trying to share with you, not simply a cold factual report. Yes, this is a blow-by-blow account, but it is in a meaningful context' (and to do that I need to turn my journalism into a work of literature).

Some stories are not fresh and flowery and full of promise and hope for mankind. They are black and ugly, but they must be told just the same, if reality is not to be sacrificed to a rosy, unreal and totally false view of life. A sincere writer must not be afraid of looking at the world as a dark place where terrible things can and do happen, as he creates an authentic human drama with vision and imagination, but without overdoing it, and in the humane service of truth, however revolting or tasteless that truth may be.

Today's beheading was sickening, horrific beyond belief and

I am still wondering how best to reveal and describe it. It stands to reason that most people do not want to know about the dark side of life unless they positively have to, because they want to enjoy their lives with a good heart and an untroubled conscience. This is entirely understandable. Who wants to live his or her life with their head down the drain? People want to have a good time, looking on the bright side for as long as possible, and not dwelling on dark and depressing things, especially if there is next to nothing they can do about such things. Life is short and they want to get on with their life and enjoy it in the best possible way. Reading about grisly and truly horrible and revolting beheadings is not exactly pleasurable for most people, who would much rather read of enjoyable and healing things of which they approve – things to uplift the spirit rather than crush it, or consign it to the doldrums. Comfort reading is what they prefer. Of course humanity still has a long way to go to achieve perfection, most people realise that perfectly well, but they do not necessarily want to be reminded of this all the time (or even part of the time!), because it is too dispiriting and/or frightening for words. It is a pain they could do without. They do not want their psyche polluted by too many messy things that are either difficult or impossible to work out. Nor do they want to be embarrassed or made to feel guilty or ashamed, or to have to think too hard about the dark side of life, which is the stuff of headaches. And who can blame them? Not me.

Even so, I will have to darken their vision for a change, if I am to tell the story of this beheading truthfully. As for my readers' shame, embarrassment, conscience, depression, displeasure, pain, messy psyche, sensitive emotions – or their addiction to a rosy view – I really cannot take any responsibility for these things, which are entirely their own affair. It is too much to ask of a writer, who could never put pen to paper if he had to take on so much of other people's emotional baggage (of which he cannot fail to be unaware, of course). He can only tell the story how it is – and in the best possible way, not crass or insensitive, but also not *weak tea and circumlocution* – and he can only hope that readers are mature and wise enough to cope with the emotional and/or political backlash and impact of his story. His readers' psycho-dynamics are not his responsibility. But, even so, it is quite a challenge.

The French Ambassador in Jeddah once said to me, 'You journalists have an enormous responsibility to get things right and not to upset the mood of your readers.' The British Ambassador once said, 'I read your article today and didn't think much of it,' to which I unhesitatingly replied, 'Then be relieved that you only had to read it. I had to write the awful stuff, which is even less pleasurable than having to read it, and I had to write it for ungrateful sods like you. But things will improve in future because, for a start, my paper will be relying far less on information and interpretation from your Embassy, which are at the root of the problem. So things can only get better.'

Having cleared the air with him, we got on like a house on fire after that!

But how to write about this truly awful, utterly ghastly, stunningly dreadful beheading?

My Saudi Arabian colleague explains that these beheadings always attract two kinds of spectator – those who turn out once and once only, in order to confirm the unbelievable, and others, such as the regulars in the crowd, who frequently turn out in order to enjoy themselves and, in the case of fanatically moral bigots, to do what they consider to be their religious duty. As I search the faces in the crowd, I can see for myself that he is not wrong. There are troubled faces that will not return again and there are remarkably untroubled smiling and laughing faces that will be back next time. Some of the laughter is probably the laughter of nervous reaction and emotional release, but there is wicked blood-lust laughter here as well – buckets of it.

Other things occur to me, too, including the fact that growing up in a desert kingdom in which terror is struck into people's hearts from a very young age – not only by public beheadings, but also by the stoning to death of adulterous women and the chopping off of thieves' hands in public places – it is impossible not to understand how to terrorise people. It is impossible not to understand what a powerful weapon terror is and how it can be used on others to such good effect, to instil terror in their hearts – it is impossible for many, maybe, not to develop the minds of terrorists. There is an inescapable culture of terror in the desert kingdom that is staring most people in the face, most of the time. So we should not be surprised if the kingdom spawns more than its fair share of terrorists.

As soon as the ambulance is on its way out of the square, escorted once more by police patrol cars and motorcycles, the executioner actually takes a little bow – a few feeble spectators clap and others remain dumb-struck – before he returns to a waiting police car which swiftly takes him on his way. This leaves adults to gossip among themselves, and excited, grinning and giggling children, many of whom have jumped up and down, and stood on tip-toe, in order to get a good look, to laugh and joke about what has taken place, which is no big deal to them as they skip away from the vulgar scene, playing their children's games.

As the crowd disperses, most people seem remarkably unsentimental and unmoved by what they have seen. Not just the Arabians, but Westerners, too – some of whom walk away with a 'so what?' shrug, while others are still laughing and joking.

Life goes on here, as elsewhere, and as the crowd disperses, my thoughts switch to the Saudi Arabian women from wealthy families seated in the overhanging balconies and galleries around the square, where they have paid through the nose for the privilege of their private boxes at the opera, so that they can enjoy the drama without mixing with the audience at street level. As I pass beneath their balconies, I can hear their long and flowing black gowns rustling like the feathers of ungainly flesh-eating vultures as they view the scene before them, waiting for the crowd to disperse from the square, before making their own decorous exit, gracious ladies that they are.

The custom is that, for something as important as a beheading, these women can drop their veils and flash their flirtatious eyes and sexy smiles – my colleague is right about that, as I discover for myself, looking up in their direction as I pass by. Their faces come eagerly and lustily alive as they watch a man's head being severed from its body, leaving the sexually frustrated young men in the crowd below to admire them from a distance and doubtless to grow hard at the thought of the women's sexual excitement burgeoning likewise, in view of the fact that these women are able, on this rare occasion, to flash the full-frontal nudity of their faces for all to see.

Phew!

One cannot fail to doubt that there is more to a Saudi Arabian beheading than meets the eyes.

Not all of those present can get themselves into a mood for

prayer afterwards, as they are expected to do, after witnessing such a shocking and soul-destroying spectacle of unashamed barbarism. I notice that a few – admittedly, not many, but some – creep off in the opposite direction away from the mosque. But the majority – who have clearly psyched themselves up for yet another blood-spattered severed head – have no difficulty in psyching themselves up for self-righteous prayer afterwards.

My Saudi Arabian colleague asks me, 'How do you feel about what you have seen?'

'Not good,' I reply, 'I think I'll go to the British Embassy to see if I can get a stiff drink at their bar.'

He laughs, 'A double gin and tonic, I suppose?'

'Yes,' I concede, 'a very large one.'

The drinking of alcohol is strictly forbidden in the desert kingdom where it is illegal to make, sell or consume it. But the Saudi Arabian Government allows foreign embassies to import their own booze if they so wish, as long as they keep it on the premises. In a country in which there are pubs with no beer, serving non-alcoholic 'near beer', apple and other fruit juices ('glasses of gloom!'), the British Embassy bar has become my local and I feel desperately in need of a drink.

'Do you feel disgusted by what you have seen?' my Arabian colleague asks.

'Of course, any civilised person would. But all countries have been there. It is impossible not to be disgusted by a great deal of history, don't you think? We, in Britain and the West, have probably severed many more heads in our time. In the United States of America, women were encouraged to turn out and watch naked black men being lynched – to see them hanging bollock-naked from trees in the deep South. There have been some proposals for *televised* executions in the electric chair in the

United States. And I wouldn't put it past one of the big US television networks to offer the Saudi authorities – if it thought that it had a chance of success – a lucrative contract for the rights to televise the desert kingdom's beheadings all over the States and around the world!'

'Will you write your own impressions of what you have seen today?'

'*The Times* has been asking me for months now for a brief report of a beheading, and an explanation of the legal and moral thinking behind it. So I shall write about today's beheading in that context. Probably not more than 500 words for the paper's international news pages.'

'But you will spare your readers the gory and sickening details, the psychological insights? You will do less than justice to the story.'

'I doubt that *The Times* will have either the space or the stomach for more than 500 words. The gory detail it will consider gratuitous.'

'But perhaps you will write a book one day, in which you can fully explain these atrocious and truly horrible matters?'

'I will do my best.'

'Remember to send me a copy, suitably disguised so that our snoopy customs officers and postal workers cannot confiscate it and report me to the police.'

'You would like to see a book written about the darker side of life in your country?'

'*Oh yes. Our elitist leaders deserve to be shamed in the outside world when they are visiting, holidaying and getting themselves educated there. They should not be allowed to keep their dirty little secrets. We shall never get any legal or social reform – any real justice or truth – in this medieval and backward country of ours unless writers expose what is going on here and explain the full horror and barbarity of it. It needs to be carefully spelled out, because we shall never put a stop to these things unless we shame our rulers into it.*

'We need to challenge and appeal to their conscience and this is impossible inside the desert kingdom where, as you know, there is no freedom either of the press or to publish too many books, which are quickly banned if the authorities feel embarrassed by them. We rely on your unashamed liberal-minded culture to examine and expose the shame of our own.'

'As I say, I'll do my best.'

'But it won't be easy for you, because I have the feeling that it is not to your taste, writing and reading about these unsavoury things.'

'Perhaps I shall rise to the occasion and not let you down. But what I have witnessed today is emotionally and mentally exhausting and now I am in urgent need of a drink. But I shall write a detailed account of this in the fullness of time, when I have had more time to digest the matter properly, after I have written my harmless, sanitised report in *The Times*. If you wish, I will show you a copy of what I have written, before I return to London. I would be interested to have your opinions.'

'Yes, please do. I would like to see how you interpret and explain all this. Will you come back and see another revolting beheading?'

'No, thank you. One is enough.'

My Saudi Arabian colleague has been schooled in the West, where he has graduated from university, and he is quite well read, so I agree to show him what I write in due course. He tells me that there are rumours that it's not only alleged murderers and rapists who are being beheaded in the desert kingdom. He has heard that the Government is ridding itself of political dissidents in this way, pretending that they are murderers and/or rapists, and he invites me to talk to exiled dissidents in London for further details.

'Do you believe that?' I ask.

'Of course. Our Government is capable of anything and what a perfectly convenient way of getting rid of dissidents. So it would not surprise me. In the absence of trial by jury in this country, nobody has any idea whether the alleged murderers and rapists are guilty of their crimes. There are no open courts in which lawyers and judges can get to the bottom of these things, and in which journalists can report on them. As you know, the press here publishes what the Government tells it to publish. So we only have the word of our dodgy princes, holy men and police for the veracity of these alleged crimes. The authorities can always bully and bribe witnesses to say whatever they want them to say, and these witnesses are never challenged or cross-examined, so it's anybody's guess whether a so-called murderer or rapist who is about to lose his head is guilty or not. Some are bound to be, of course, but by no means all who lose their heads are guilty. This is a place where you can lose your head for being innocent, for having a face that does not fit.'

In *The Times*, my report appears under the heading RUTHLESS JUSTICE DEFENDS SOCIAL STRUCTURE, and it explains that the application of criminal justice in the desert kingdom is swift and ruthless. The Saudi Government is extremely pleased with the report in 'the top people's paper', because I take care to explain that, by definition, a crime under Islamic law is a forbidden act, or the abandonment of a command. So all forbidden acts and commands – directly from or

influenced by the Koran and its interpretation by holy men –
are punishable.

Because punishment and retaliation are the keynotes in an
ancient culture that is based on the tried and presumed true
proposition that, without religiously inspired criminal
punishment, the whole structure of society will be
permanently impaired, Saudi Arabian believers will quote
from the Koran as follows: 'In punishment, there is life for
you, O people of understanding,' and 'There is life for you in
retaliation, O man of understanding, that you may guard
yourself.'

Punishment is commonly regarded as both a deterrent and
a corrective – and when, in the belief of the Koran, the crime
violates other people's rights or socio-religious institutions –
then the punishment prescribed is unashamedly and
wholeheartedly severe. These are no-nonsense punishments
for full-blooded men and women. The worst crimes for which
maximum punishments are prescribed are intentional murder
and rape, the penalty for which is beheading in a place of
public execution. But one can also be executed for the sin of
apostasy! Can you believe that? To be executed for abandoning
one's religious faith and refusing to believe in God is quite
something, isn't it?

Shouldn't the United Nations be concerned about this?
Shouldn't there be a discussion or debate about it? Shouldn't
somebody do something about this? What if an atheist comes
to the desert kingdom, without realising that he can have his
head chopped off for apostasy? Shouldn't governments in the
outside world talk to the rulers of the desert kingdom about
this? In Holland, one mullah has called for the execution of
Dutch homosexuals, and this is one pernicious thought that

has not reached the desert kingdom as yet ... a good thing, too, in a land in which homosexuality is secretly widely practised.

In the case of murder, if the next-of-kin or 'person suffering' from the death of the murder victim forgives the murderer, then he may be given a remission and save his head under the law, with 'blood money' paid by way of compensation for the life he has taken.

In addition to murder and rape, capital punishment can also be prescribed for stealing, depending on the circumstances. The Koran recommends that 'the punishment for those who wage war against God and His Messenger and strive to make mischief in the land is only this, that they should be put to death, or crucified, or their hands and feet should be cut off on opposite sides, or they should be imprisoned. This shall be as a disgrace for them in this world and in the hereafter they shall have grievous chastisement.'

The leaving of a thief's body on a crucifix in a public place is seen as a deterrent to others with stealing in mind.

Because all this is properly and fully explained in my report in *The Times*, the Saudi Government is pleased to have got its message over. It feels that too many Westerners do not properly understand the serious religious and highly moral thinking that underlies its policy in these criminal matters. It feels that too many are ignorant of the culture of the desert kingdom, so it looks forward to more reports of this kind from my pen.

Other religiously inspired severe punishments, applying to other crimes in the desert kingdom, are also explained in my report, and are dealt with later in this collection.

There are two points of view in Saudi Arabia today. There is the hard-headed, hard-hearted viewpoint of the fund-amentalists and traditionalists, who believe in the clenched-fist merits and virtues of severe and savage punishments. And then there is the more liberal perspective of social reformers such as my colleague, who believe in a more humane and modern interpretation of the desert kingdom's ancient laws and traditions, and about which not very much is heard. There may also be a fanatical silent majority that puts the fear of hell into the traditionalists and frightens them into sticking to their severe punishments. We have seen these fanatics in the Middle East before. We have seen them in our own history before. Nothing is new, not in history, not in this part of the world, not anywhere.

Months after the public beheading that I witnessed, I am showing my Saudi colleague a copy of my discourse on this subject. In the meantime, I have toughened up, as a result of seeing, and also hearing about other equally barbaric and sickening practices from eyewitnesses, so I am no longer squeamish about putting pen to paper. I hope that I have achieved an impressionistic and personalised account that is as moral as it is realistic and factual.

After a long and thoughtful pause, he takes a deep breath and tells me: 'This is very powerful and perceptive. The stuff of nightmares, I dare say. You have caught the atmosphere exactly and I like your mood. Your story has a crystal-clear ring of truth about it. You have the authority to write this. You have been here and seen things with your own eyes. I really hope you publish it when you return to London.'

Such stories are not to everybody's taste, of course, but, as the novelist D. H. Lawrence once remarked, 'We write a novel or two, we are called … depraved, or idiotic, or boring. What does it matter, we go the road just the same.'

Most roads in the desert kingdom lead to dark and depraved places.

2

WOMEN ARE ALWAYS
TO BLAME

A distraught and hysterical woman, her deeply anguished and petrified face hidden inside her *burka*, is dragged shrieking from her home in an Arabian village where she has been ostracised. Her screams of terror fill the hot desert air. Hers are the paralysing shrieks of a woman fraught with deadly fear, to ring in the ears of her neighbours and haunt them for ever, to haunt us all for ever.

Some neighbours have come out of their houses to watch her as she is dragged through the streets, kicking and screaming, in the shameful direction of the central village square where she is taken by the strong arm of the law, in the form of two policemen with psychopathic grins on their faces, who easily overpower her as they manhandle her in the direction of her ugly fate. There is panic in the air. The woman is panic-stricken, as are those who are close to her, or feel for her even though they hardly know her. But we all know this woman, we can recognise her well enough, she is close to our hearts, and we cannot fail to be concerned for her.

Not all of her neighbours turn out to watch. Some stay at home with their doors firmly locked, too ashamed to show their faces, too depressed and sickened by what is about to happen, unable to watch what they are powerless to prevent. The dreadful plight of this poor defenceless woman, which they cannot put out of their minds, has sickened them to the pit of their stomachs, and they are truly depressed to the roots of their being, consumed with a collective guilt under the bright sun of a clear-blue desert sky. They feel guilty for not daring to object, for not having the courage to fight against what is happening to this woman, for letting her be dragged away against her and their will to meet her death. They cannot bear to think about the disgusting and barbaric nature of the death that awaits her. It is mind-boggling and beyond belief. The gory details are too distressing and shaming.

She does not deserve this – no one on earth deserves this – yet she is following in the footsteps of a number of women who similarly did not deserve such an atrocious and cruelly unjust fate at the hands of their men, while the rest of the world just stood by.

And that's exactly what the rest of the world does, it just stands by and watches; or stands by and does not watch, either because it does not know, or does not want to know, or because it feels unable or disinclined, like this woman's neighbours, to do anything about what it knows. Perhaps it stands by in a dumbfounded outrage that it doesn't know how to express in the face of such an unspeakably atrocious offence against women everywhere. Perhaps it conveniently looks the other way and puts this woman out of sight and mind, because it cannot bring itself to watch what it feels powerless to do anything about.

Some of this woman's neighbours do not regard her fate as unspeakable at all. On the contrary, they think that she richly deserves her treatment and they intend to gloat, and feast their eyes upon it, so that they can talk and gossip about it for the rest of their lives, as a warning to other such women of what will happen to them if they should cheat on their husbands, as it is said that she has done. They will speak loudly of her sinful crime, which outrages and disgusts them so much that they believe that no punishment could be too cruel or terrible enough for her. You name it and she deserves it, in their view. They are without compassion or conscience, because to them she is a piece of filth, a worthless slut who is no longer fit for decent male or female company. So she must, of course, be put to death in public, in full view of her neighbours, for everyone to see what happens to such shamefully unclean women who are not fit to live on the same earth as the rest of us.

Such women are no better than dung beetles or cockroaches that should be stamped upon and squashed under foot, before they spread their germs. The world must be cleansed of them, and so it is in the desert kingdom, the land of the pure, where few would dare to mourn such hated women, not openly, and perhaps not even in secret, for fear of being found out and reported to the authorities. Such women must be expunged and in such a way as to terrify and deter all other married women from cheating on their husbands. They must be stoned to death, by other women, and by their men, and by children, too, if they have the physical strength with which to match the greater strength of moral purpose of their role models, the adults, as they hurl their stones and rocks at an adulterous woman until she is well and truly stone dead.

The central square is cleared and swept clean for the occasion. All exits are blocked by policemen and a pile of stones and rocks has been dumped in one corner of the square for members of the public to take their pick. Today, villagers are only allowed to enter the square if they are prepared to participate in the stoning, either as stone-throwers, or as spectators who boo and hiss – spectators who carefully position themselves behind the stone-throwers, whom they do their best to shadow, for fear of being hit themselves, by any stray stones or rocks that might come in their direction. It is an ancient, wide and spacious square, devoid of any glass windows, or properties that can be damaged. If it were otherwise, this stoning would be held out in the desert, away from the village. Apart from the solid walls and heavy wooden doors of the properties around the square, which can easily withstand the impact of an occasional stone or rock, there is nothing at stake, other than the adulterous woman's life. The square is also wide and long enough for the woman not to be able to run very far before her pursuers catch up with her and fell her with their missiles. She is easy meat. If she runs at all, she will not get farther than a few yards at most. She will be quickly hunted down.

In addition to those who hunt her in the square, there are more spectators on rooftops, many of whom have stones and rocks of their own, which they will hurl in her direction if she draws near on their side of the square.

The scene is set for the adulterous woman to enter the square, and her arrival is announced by her terrified screams and shrieks which can be heard from a distance, becoming louder as she and the policemen draw near, as she is dragged through the streets, whilst others hold their breath.

It is not the first time that an adulterous woman has been stoned to death in this square and it may not be the last. But, in some villages, there are no stonings at all, because married women do not dare to risk an adulterous liaison. In other villages, there is perhaps not more than one stoning in most people's lifetime. Few records are kept of these grisly events, and those that are kept are not available for public scrutiny. They are known only to a handful of shadowy people who keep an eye on the chastity of women in the desert kingdom, who have it in their power not to disclose any information at all if they do not feel inclined to do so. They also have it in their power to doctor, destroy or mislay such information, and since they are not always the most competent of people, sometimes the information is genuinely mislaid or lost.

But however many women have been stoned to death in recent times – dozens, hundreds or thousands, it makes no difference – they won't go away simply because the desert kingdom gets shot of them with stones and rocks. On the contrary, they will haunt the kingdom and stain its honour forever. All the perfumes of Arabia will not remove the stain or the stench.

These women are victims of our own deafness – the deafness of a kingdom that does not wish to hear, or shed a single tear on their behalf, and the deafness of the outside world that hears even less. They are the saddest and most tragic of all the ghosts that haunt the Arabian sands, for their crime has been to have loved and to have engendered so much poisonous and lethal hate as a result, so much sexual and moral fear, so many perverse and deadly passions.

When the authorities cannot find enough people to turn out and stone an adulterous woman – either because the population is too old and infirm in villages where only a handful of people live, or because whole families have mysteriously disappeared on the appointed day – they are happy to execute her with the aid of a tipper-truck instead, the back of which can be raised hydraulically from a horizontal to a near vertical position, in order to empty its contents from the back, letting them slide swiftly to the ground in an avalanche. Piled high with rocks and stones, these rugged trucks are used in the desert kingdom to tip their contents on to adulterous women, positioned behind the vehicle in a crouching position, directly below the avalanche of rocks and stones, which crush the victims to death.

The women are made to crouch behind the trucks by 'brave' policemen who fearlessly surround the women on all sides, making sure that they cannot cause the truck driver any problems by moving out of the line of fire. On such occasions, women are killed more quickly, so their pain is less prolonged than when they are stoned to death by their peers. It is also said that sometimes women are buried up to their necks in sand, so that their heads can be stoned, or confined to a pit in which they can meet their fate. Some are stoned with smaller stones to ensure a slow death and to prolong their pain.

But today it is an angry mob that will do the business in this square and it should not be forgotten that it is not only the body of a woman that will be stoned here. Her emotions will be crushed as well. It is her heart's delight – the love of a good woman. These too will be bruised and stoned and have their life crushed out of them. The nearness and awful danger and terrible expectation of pain invokes and accelerates deadly fear, a truly horrible emotion for any defenceless victim to experience at the brink of death, and when this emotion is churned up with the sharp feeling of injustice and insult, it is, of course, acutely painful. This is the kind of fear that is all-encompassing and utterly devastating and it can sink you like a heavy rock. This is a fear to pulverise the stoutest heart.

So, when a woman is stoned to death for something as relatively harmless by Western standards and, perhaps, even understandable, as adultery – while adulterous men go unpunished because, in the desert kingdom, it is women who are always to blame – then she feels a bruising and crushing sense of injustice along with the heavy weight of insult in her soul, to add to the painful crushing of her own bones.

Not that anyone cares about such a woman's soul, as she is buried, not only under a heap of stones and rocks, but under an awful and crushing feeling of deeply wounding insult, fear and mental anxiety, as she goes needlessly to her death. There is fear of pain that takes its time with her body, as one stone or rock follows another, slowly butchering her, and there is also fear of being maimed, deformed, disfigured and mutilated.

Then there is fear of being completely and utterly without hope or compassion or mercy or understanding, or help, or justice, or the basic human rights to which anyone may reasonably feel entitled. Added to all this is the fear of death itself, and it becomes an unbearable burden. The mental anguish and paralysing distress is as destructive as the stones and rocks.

In a world in which many countries are concerned about cruelty to animals – about cruelty to race horses owned by Arab princes – it is odd, to say the least, that there is such little concern over the cruel and brutal fate of the desert kingdom's adulterous and allegedly adulterous women.

'What,' an adulterous woman may ask herself and anybody else who is remotely interested, 'have I done to deserve this? What have I done that is so bad and despicable and wicked that I deserve such a cruel fate as this?'

Not that she will be sufficiently conscious or clear-sighted for such speculation as her dislocated mind and body – her life itself – disappear before what is left of her eyes under the blizzard of stones and rocks that rain down on her, as these missiles take her apart piece by piece for the morbid curiosity and satisfaction of the crowd, as she longs for the relief of death, as she longs for the next stone or rock to put her out of her desperate misery, or a tipper-truck to protect her from the angry mob.

Suddenly, the angry mob enters the square, following the two policemen who are dragging the despised and hysterical woman into it, while people shout their abuse at her. And just as suddenly there is silence when the woman faints, collapsing on the ground. She is scooped up by the policemen and carried to the centre of the square where she is unceremoniously dumped, while the mob makes its thoughtful and chilling way to the pile of rocks and stones that has been reserved for it.

The woman does not regain consciousness, so there is something of an anti-climax, now that the mob is denied the high drama of the chase. She just lies there on the ground, with the hot and merciless sun beating down on her, as the unforgiving mob approaches, armed with its stones and rocks, while spectators also pour into the square and on to the rooftops, lining it on all sides. The policemen do nothing to revive the woman. Instead, they beckon the ground-level spectators to come closer, so that they can get a better view of her and the mob that is poised to stone her.

Then the policemen give the OK to kill her off, which the fanatical mob proceeds to do, taking it in turns to throw their stones and rocks at her at virtual point-blank range, watching the gradual disfigurement and butchery of her body.

There are no more shrieks and screams. Only a few moans and groans, in addition to the sounds of her body being maimed and crushed – the soft thudding sounds of a melon or marrow being struck by a hammer as her head is repeatedly hit, time and again; the grinding and splintering sound of glass, or of a hard carrot being broken, snapped and chopped by a sharp kitchen knife, as her skull, fingers, ribs, cheek and jaw bones are broken; the soft squashing and bursting sound of tomatoes being thrown against a wall, as her skin and flesh disintegrate; the dull thud of a boiled potato or egg being thrown against a wall, as the flesh of her breasts is destroyed; the chop, chop, chopping sound of a woodcutter or the sound of the splintering and snapping of plywood, as her neck and spine are slowly broken in several places; the squidge and crunch of vegetables in a blender, and the crunchy sound of biscuits under a rolling pin, as all her remaining bones are pulverised.

Most people cannot imagine how it sounds when a woman is being stoned to death. Whilst they can imagine her terrified shrieks and screams, her anguished and deeply distressed moans and groans, they cannot imagine what the stones and rocks sound like on impact.

Hearing a woman being stoned to death is as bad as seeing her. Both are seriously sickening beyond belief, as is the ghastly sight of a crowd of morbid spectators and stone-throwers in their unashamed degradation.

But what does such a woman hear and feel as she goes to her grave?

Fortunately, she is spared the horrifying sight of seeing herself – since her eyes, if they are still open, are focused on the mob – but she can, no doubt, fleetingly imagine what she must look like, as the stones and rocks come at her from all directions, and what is left of her imaginings flash across her anguished mind at the point of death.

But most of all she can hear the harrowing sounds of her own destruction in her ears, as her body is torn apart and butchered. It is these sounds – along with the choking and gurgling sound of her own blood, and the heavy breathing of her own fear lost in the blood-lust of the angry mob – that she takes with her to the grave, as she wonders what on earth she can have done to deserve such a barbarous and inhumane fate, such an unjust death, that is as heart-breaking and gut-wrenching as it is bone-crushing.

The square is now empty, the crowd and the stone-throwers having dispersed and gone back to their homes, and the police having scooped up the remains of the woman's body and tossed them into the back of a truck that has arrived to take them away. The square is empty until the next time, as are other squares, somewhere in the desert kingdom, where the outside world is not looking, and does not dare to look.

3

THIEVES ARE ALWAYS HANDICAPPED

I never saw a man with a more hangdog expression than the one who lost his right hand outside the *souk* today, where a small crowd gathered to watch as his hand was painfully severed from his arm, above the wrist, and then taken away and tossed on to some scrap heap somewhere or other in this bizarre city. I never saw a man more mesmerised by his own hand, or a face so despairing of a ruthless and mind-boggling system of justice that thinks nothing of chopping off a man's hand for stealing on three occasions, that thinks nothing of making him bare his arm in public, stretched out on a sturdy table, serving as a chopping block, for an axe to fall upon it. I never saw a man so hypnotised by what was about to happen to him, whose attention and will were so psychologically paralysed by a single, horrifying thought. I never saw a man so severely punished for having stolen goodness knows what on at least three occasions.

Thieves in Saudi Arabia who steal three times or more are liable to have their hands chopped off to teach them the lesson that thieving is wicked and will not be tolerated; less prolific thieves and pickpockets are simply imprisoned where they are doubtless flogged. A man who steals only three times can lose his hand, and should his thieving become habitual – should he become a life-long thief, stealing, say, 33 or 300 times – he can lose both hands if he is found out and convicted.

Whilst no starving person can be punished for stealing food in the desert kingdom, for any other theft, robbers, thieves, muggers, burglars, pickpockets and handbag-snatchers are all severely punished, as a result of which there doesn't seem to be much of this type of crime in evidence, because a sure way to stop a thief is to deprive him of the tools of his trade – his hand or hands. But there are still some thieves who remain undeterred and carry on thieving at the risk of losing a hand if they do not keep their wits about them. A lenient judge may possibly let a third conviction pass without amputation, but there are those who are not so lenient.

With common consent, the desert kingdom of Saudi Arabia is a place like no other. It is the kind of place where you can be minding your own business, strolling through a *souk* and thinking about nothing in particular, when, all of a sudden, you come upon a man who is having his hand amputated before a crowd of spectators, from which you can either avert your gaze, as you hurry away in the opposite direction, or you can stand and stare with everybody else, as astonishment and disbelief suddenly wash over you.

That's the sort of fraught and unsettling place the desert kingdom is. You turn a corner when, suddenly, you are confronted by something extremely unpleasant, when you find yourself bang up against something that makes you think very seriously and carefully about life and your own part in it, about where you are heading, and whether you ought to be watching the horrifying spectacle before you, whether you ought to be getting the next flight out.

Listen ... nobody is in favour of stealing, that goes without saying. Nobody approves of burglars and thieves, robbers and muggers, some of whom are deeply unpleasant and violent, while others are simply pathetic and not in the least dangerous criminals. Nobody can turn a blind eye to the personal and social problems they cause, some of whom may steal out of desperation and need. Everybody agrees that they must be dealt with and punished. Of course they must. But the punishment must fit the crime, and nobody can convince me that amputating a man's hand in a needlessly savage manner, in a public place for the purpose of spectacle, is a proper punishment that fits the crime of a person who may only have stolen on three separate occasions. In this day and age, such a punishment cannot be right.

But the desert kingdom of Saudi Arabia is *not in this day and age*, it is in another period of time entirely, a medieval and backward period of time where we have also been in our history, before we civilised ourselves out of it. But the Saudis show no sign of doing this as we embark on the new millennium. Many, if not most Saudis, for all their modernity, money, Western architecture and trendy designer clothes, are still medieval under the skin. Their hearts are still medieval and they are very comfortable with this, these people of past and present, with a foot in both camps, who can carry out this savagery and vengeance completely without conscience.

The Saudis could stop these barbaric punishments tomorrow.

There is nothing to stop them. But they do not choose to do so because they do, as it happens, believe in them. So what's it to us? That's what they say. Who are we to preach to them, when they take care not to preach to us about the system of justice in our country, or anything else for that matter?

'It's not our business ...' we both say, time and again.

For all their fabulous wealth and opportunities for advancement, the Saudis have no intention of ridding themselves of their vicious past. They are keeping it on the back burner and applying it to the modern world as and when it suits them to do so, and if their European and Western allies don't like it, well, they can lump it. And lumping it is what Saudi Arabia's allies are having to do, which is why they would rather not talk or read too much about this, because they feel highly embarrassed and ashamed to find themselves accepting such morally despicable acts, for the sake of economics and oil.

In a way, the West's double standards – turning a blind eye and tolerating barbaric punishments inside the desert kingdom where there is serious money to be made, whilst not tolerating such barbarism or savage justice in their own more civilised and liberal-minded home countries – is racist. This is because it clearly demonstrates what the West, hand on heart, actually thinks but dare not say about – or to the face of – Saudi Arabia and other such countries. And what it secretly thinks is that the desert kingdom is an uncivilised and barbarous country where it is acceptable for the natives to be beheaded, flogged and have their hands chopped off, and acceptable for women to be stoned to death as long as the oil keeps flowing in a Westerly direction and Western workers can still find jobs there. But it is not in the least acceptable for Europeans or North Americans to suffer such inhumane punishments, because they are, of course, far too superior for that sort of thing. They are lucky enough to live in much more civilised countries.

If this is not what the West secretly thinks, then why does it remain silent about such truly horrible and inhumane things that it would not allow in the Western world? Why doesn't it protest, as it does in other parts of the world, where it has nothing to lose and when it disapproves morally of what is happening there? How come it doesn't table resolutions at the United Nations? Because Saudi Arabia and other such places have the West over a barrel of oil, that's why.

Clearly, the Saudis have the West over a barrel in more ways than one. It started with a barrel of oil, but the implications are much wider than oil.

The thief in the *souk* is still waiting patiently to have his hand chopped off. And what is worse is that it will be his right hand. Of course, it is difficult to eat without one's right hand, not only in Saudi Arabia, but anywhere else in the world, where eating with the left hand in the absence of the right can be a problem. But it is a much bigger problem in the desert kingdom, because people are not supposed to eat with their left hand, and the reason for this is because their scriptures tell them that the left hand must be reserved for wiping their bottoms, and is not to be used for any other purpose! Strictly speaking, because they are not allowed to eat with the same hand with which they clean themselves, they can only ever use their right hand. Cutting off the hand that a thief uses for eating, and compelling him thereby to eat with his bottom-cleaning hand in future – which is highly offensive to him and to others – is a deliberate humiliation, well calculated to remind him and others that he is unclean, a despised and stigmatised piece of filth, who must spend the rest of his life eating with his forbidden hand, although the Saudis claim that, since he stole with his right hand, it is logical to take the right, but the trouble with this argument is that most thieves steal with both hands.

It is with this odious contempt that the Saudi authorities sanction the cutting off of a thief's right hand instead of his left; they wish to remind him that he is to pay heavily for his thieving ways, as they show him no mercy whatsoever.

With his bare arm outstretched on the table, as he sat there in a chair, guarded by policemen, I never saw a man looking more dismal, downcast and mournful, as he took a last look at his hand, and studied his hairy arm, so full of life, so warm with life-giving blood and full of strength, so muscular and well crafted, so relaxed, with skin that was about to be split and torn to the bone under a sharp axe, cutting its way through the ample flesh, veins and arteries, and crushing and breaking the bone of his arm in two.

I never saw a man look so shame-faced, but almost in a resigned and indifferent way, as if to suggest that the loss of his hand and wrist was, when all was said and done, of no real consequence any more. No doubt his apparent indifference was born of necessity and inevitability – a necessary defensive reaction to an inevitable and inescapable punishment from which he knew there was no escape, in his inevitable and impoverished life, performing his ill-fated role as a thief, either to relieve his poverty, or to enjoy just a few of the modest pleasures that would not otherwise come his way.

'What has he stolen?' I asked an English-speaking Saudi in the crowd.

'Some expensive watches,' he replied, ' the police say they caught him in the act on the third occasion and that there is no doubt that he was the one who stole some other valuable watches on two previous occasions, not from the same shop, but from other shops. He is a very guilty man who has confessed to his crime, from which he has profited very well from the cash that he has raised on the black market from his ill-gotten gains. He must not be allowed to think that his crimes are not serious, because they are very serious indeed and will not be tolerated. We have a very low crime rate in this country, thanks in no small measure to the severity of our punishments. We do not take a lenient or philosophical view of criminals, as you do in your country.'

'How many watches has he stolen?' I enquired, 'and how much did he make on the black market?'

'How much did he make?' he echoed in disbelief. ' Who can tell? I don't know. The police did not say.'

'Shall we ask them?'

'Better not. Better to keep out of it. We don't want them to think that we are associated or interested in any possible way. Best to steer clear of the police in this country. They are not "user-friendly" and they might think that we, too, are planning to steal some watches, if we ask questions about their value on the black market! The police are not amenable to questions from members of the public. Where are you from? Great Britain?'

'Yes, from London.'

'Ah, London. I love that city. I have had *such* good times there. And the English are such nice people. I was a student there. So many beautiful women, I could hardly believe my eyes, and so available. My God, to be back in London again! With all those lovely women everywhere. Have you been here long?'

'Just over a year. I shall be returning to London shortly.'

'Have you enjoyed your stay here?'

'In a manner of speaking,' I lied and then thought that it

wasn't a complete lie, because there were some things that I had enjoyed, even though, on balance, the enjoyable things had been completely swamped by the deeply unpleasant, deadly dull and boring things. And it is also the case that, in a manner of speaking, an investigative journalist does enjoy investigating.

'In a manner of speaking,' he laughed out loud, 'that's good, very good indeed.'

Suddenly, a medic appeared on the scene, together with an axe-man, who immediately took up the axe from the table and examined its cutting edge. Time was running out for the man who stole watches, who was still looking very lugubrious and deeply unhappy. Here was a man whose controlled emotions were turning this way and that, like a revolving weather-vane, between an apparent indifference to his inevitable fate and a feeling of mounting fear and anxiety. Here was a man doing his best to keep his fear at arm's length, as he sat there looking up at us under a fevered brow.

I wondered whether he would be given a pain-killing injection, or a tranquilliser maybe, as happens in some instances, but apparently not on this occasion, because I could see no such medication. I wondered whether they would blindfold the poor devil to spare him the ghastly and hideous sight of his own arm being severed above the wrist, of his own blood spurting and spitting in his face, as his hand was cast to one side. Maybe they wanted him to see his own blood, to see how easily they detached his thieving hand from his arm. Maybe they would force him to watch what they were doing to him in order to show their contempt and to increase the severity of his horror and his pain.

There were bandages aplenty on a second table, so they seemed well equipped to patch him up afterwards, but how will this man endure it all? Will he faint when or before the axe falls? Will he grit his teeth and get through it all, as he wavers between indifference and fear, relying on the former to overcome the latter. If only someone would give him a tranquilliser or anaesthetic, but there is, it seems, no hope of that. If only his minders would comfort him in some way. On the contrary, they are laughing at and about him, his police guards, laughing to hide their shame, maybe, these miserable specimens of human beings, these cruel and callous men who seem to be enjoying what they have come here to do.

The convicted criminal clenches and unclenches his prone fist, curling and releasing his fingers like one trying to rid himself of pins and needles. The axe-man stands by, waiting to get this amputation over and done with. He shifts around and glances at the policemen for a sign from them to get on with it. Two of the policemen have gripped the thief firmly by his shoulders, while a third is ordering him to reach out and grip the far edge of the table and hold firmly to it. I have heard that, in some cases, the man's arm is strapped down.

'They are going to do it now,' declared the English-speaking Saudi whose acquaintance I had made in the crowd.

'I don't think I really want or need to see any more of this,' I said to myself. 'I think I've had enough, seen enough for my purpose.'

The thief who is about to lose his hand is still looking troubled but implacable for all that and his face, firmly set against what is about to be done to him, is still giving very little away. I doubt that too many people in this crowd are all that interested in his face, in the subtleties of expression and the shades of grey in his dark brown eyes.

I hear a loud gasp from the crowd as I force myself once more to witness the scene, and I see an axe falling precisely on target, and a hand severed under a shower of blood, and a man who has fainted.

Whether he fainted before or after the fall of the axe, I cannot tell. Clearly, he must be in a state of profound shock from this savage blow to his body – to his nervous system – and who is to say whether he has had a heart-attack, or strained the muscles of his heart in some way as a result of the terrible shock. But one thing's for sure – he will never be able to use his precious hand again.

This time I really am ready to leave, as the rest of the crowd stays on watching a medic hurriedly treating and bandaging the gaping wound at the bottom of the man's arm, just above the wrist.

4

Lash 'Em and
Flog 'Em

When a man is lashed with a thin cane with razor-sharp edges – cutting into his skin like a whip, clawing his flesh like a pointed barbed-wire spike – he experiences profound physical pain and mental agony, as his skin splinters and cracks open on his bare back, as it is criss-crossed with streams of blood.

When a man's stinging sweat seeps its salt into his wounds, into his split skin, his gritted teeth and exhausted nerves are on a knife edge, as he is struck time and again with a thin, sharp and willowy cane, bending this way and that, carving up his back like there is no tomorrow. Such a man is emotionally and physically destroyed from such an assault.

Some men's backs are cherry red and almost ripped to shreds when they are thrashed to within an inch of their lives. Others don't do too badly, if they are administered only a few strikes.

But what do these men do to deserve this punishment, which is generally performed in public? Their crime is to drink, make or deal in illegal alcohol – while their superiors, princes and wealthy sheikhs, drink as much alcohol as they like, in the safety of their palaces and homes. These guilty men may also have been involved in fights, drunken or hooligan behaviour, or may have defied the authorities somehow. They may also have been caught practising a forbidden religion in private, if they are not Muslims.

If you're not careful, you can be lashed for all manner of activities in the desert kingdom. It depends on the mood of the authorities and their policemen.

Perpetrators can receive just a few gentle and relatively harmless lashes if the authorities happen to be in a good mood and take a lenient view, or a lethal number of lashes can be prescribed over a period of time, because the victims will not be able to take them all in one go, and survive to tell the tale.

During the construction of a new airport at Abhar in the south of Saudi Arabia, a young British bulldozer operator – George Cain, from London – committed suicide in a Saudi jail when he discovered that, having served six months behind bars already, he would have to serve another six months in return for the withdrawal of 120 lashes that had been handed down to him as a part of his sentence.

One hundred and twenty lashes are virtually unbearable. They comprise the maximum possible sentence. A dozen are no joke, but 120 are at least 100 too many. It's a lot of punishment to suffer and it takes a physically and mentally strong man to endure it.

But George Cain's lashes were waived at the request of the British Embassy when it pointed out that it would not be good for Saudi–British relations if a British subject were to be sentenced under Saudi law to be severely lashed. The Embassy also argued that a sentence of 120 vicious lashes – to be administered in regular beatings every six weeks in front of other employees at the airbase – might conceivably result in the death of a man. After haggling for six months, the Saudi authorities finally relented, but not without insisting that George Cain, who had already served six months behind bars, should serve a further six months if they could no longer lash him, as they had been eagerly looking forward to doing.

This meant that George Cain could only escape his lashes by agreeing to serve a total of 12 months in jail. The thought of doing yet another six months was too much for the young man. As a result, he just snapped, putting his head into a plastic bag and suffocating himself to death, after leaving a suicide note for his father back in England. Clearly, little thought had been given to his mental state.

But what had been his crime? He had got drunk on illegal booze – *sidiki* – and deliberately driven his bulldozer into the site office at the airport where he worked. He did this out of mounting frustration leading to an explosion of anger, as he'd been kept waiting for an exit visa for many weeks, a visa that he had requested in order to leave the desert kingdom, after he had been sacked by his employers. The Saudi authorities, who move at a snail's pace most of the time, can play cat and mouse with a person's application for an exit visa, and often they seem to delight in doing so.

Back in London, when I wrote about George Cain's suicide for the *Daily Express*, my article didn't raise an eyebrow – the attitude was 'that's Saudi Arabia for you', and so it is. If the Saudi authorities were given the task of sorting out Europe's soccer hooligans, the chances are there would be no hooligans.

But as if to excuse themselves for using the lash – sometimes for quite trivial transgressions – the Saudi authorities claim that lashing is not as bad as is made out, and that flogging is much worse. They argue that they never flog anyone with a lethal rod, cord or rope, and they seem to believe that their willowy, sharp-edged canes are really quite civilised. They seem to think that it is very considerate of them to agree to beat a man with nothing more damaging than a razor-sharp cane.

But there are rumours from visitors to Saudi jails – and from prisoners inside those jails – that heavy flogging does occur in the desert kingdom, carried out by twisted prison guards behind locked doors, where brutal tortures are also undertaken.

But the point is not whether lashing with canes is not as bad as flogging with rods, cords or ropes. Such questions are academic when what the Saudis ought really to be asking themselves is whether any of these cruel punishments are justified – whether any of them fit the crime. It stands to reason that a sound lashing with a razor-sharp cane is going to cause serious harm and injury, while not more than a few strikes, gently administered, are perhaps not going to do too much harm, and the Saudis argue that the severity of the lashings depends on the severity of the crime – an eye for an eye. But the higher and more humane question is whether these lashings are necessary at all.

No doubt, these punishments by cruel caning pale into insignificance when compared with beheadings, the chopping off of hands, and the stoning to death of adulterous women, but a bloodthirsty lashing remains an inhumane and barbaric remedy none the less.

I once saw a European nurse having her legs gently lashed to teach her a lesson for being foolhardy enough to wear a very short mini-skirt that showed far too much leg and thigh in downtown Jeddah.

And I once attended a house party to celebrate the departure of the daughter of a Sheikh. She was leaving the desert kingdom for Cambridge University in England, and while I was at her farewell party, a young Arabian schoolgirl – in the same mountain village of Taif where the party was being held in the Sheikh's summer house – was being expelled from her school because she had said in an interview in a local Arabic newspaper that she was 'in love' with a Saudi pop singer.

This young schoolgirl was expelled by the Director of Religious Education on the grounds that she was a wicked and sinful little girl who would contaminate the morals of other girls in her class. At the same time, the Sheikh's high-born daughter was merrily playing her guitar and singing Western pop songs for the benefit of her guests – foreign diplomats and others, including the British Ambassador – while wearing a delightful dress with plunging neckline that showed plenty of cleavage. Unlike the European nurse who showed too much leg and thigh, the Sheikh's daughter was not in danger of being lashed for alleged indecency, but other women in the desert kingdom were.

It was a charming party and the charismatic and world-famous Sheik was an equally charming host. He ladled some soup into a bowl for me and discussed the civilised pleasures of being in England.

5

INSTITUTIONALISED SLAVERY AND RACISM

The British and Americans – who did not, of course, invent the slave trade – abolished slavery in 1833 and 1863 respectively. But the Saudi Arabians dragged their feet until the following century when, as recently as 1962, they finally and reluctantly got around to emancipating an estimated 4,000 of the desert kingdom's slaves. A staggering 129 years after the abolition of slavery by the British, the Saudi Arabians finally and reluctantly get the message.

The penny drops, painfully slowly, when Saudis grudgingly agree at last with the United Nations, the outside world and human rights conventions that slavery is dreadfully and morally wrong, as if they never knew it in the first place, as if they could not be expected to know such an incredible thing, as if news of the emancipation of slaves in the outside world had not reached them, in their isolated little backwater, for

129 years. It really is incredible by any standard or stretch of the imagination.

The Saudi attitude to this day would seem to be how could they possibly have been expected to know that it was wrong? 'It never occurred to us, really it didn't. As for immoral ... well, don't mention such complicated matters, it was never immoral in our view – we would not have done it otherwise – and isn't it true that some of our life-long slaves were content to stay put after abolition?' ... having been rendered so utterly useless and demoralised by their enslavement for so long.

Slavery, indeed – why, most people in the land of the pure always thought that it was the most natural and harmless thing on God's earth. They always thought that there was nothing essentially wrong with the practice at all. They actually thought that they were doing their slaves a big favour, snatching and protecting them from a harsh world, and treating them like household pets. Yes, that's how they saw it, or so they will tell you.

The ancient Greeks and Romans did it, didn't they? The ancient Chinese and Mongolians did it. And the black Africans were doing it all along. Adolf Hitler did it. So what's the problem? Has the modern world gone mad? Slavery is as old as the hills – or the desert sands, if you like – so why all this latter-day fuss about it?

It is no exaggeration to say that this is a typical Saudi Arabian train of thought, in a country in which people have been extremely reluctant to abolish slavery until relatively recent times. Saudi Arabians always demonstrated their liking for the morally abhorrent slave trade, which they never failed to administer without conscience and with a great deal of enthusiasm. 1962!

Think about it. It's unbelievable. The mind boggles. No wonder people say there is nowhere else like Saudi Arabia (unless they happen to be slaves).

As anyone who has travelled extensively in the desert kingdom knows, most Saudis are natural-born racists, who regard themselves as white rather than black or brown, and who don't lose any sleep about enslaving 'lesser breeds'. It's the 'higher' white breeds that they prefer and, good and kindly fascists that they so obviously are, they have no great objection to a spot of slavery on the side, or in a good cause.

Enslaving others is part of the desert kingdom's history, you see. It's in its blood, which is why these marvellous people held out against the abolition of slavery longer than any other country in the world. They have an excellent record of defiance in this regard. They stood by their racist views and defended them and their slave trade in the face of worldwide criticism. They – like the British at the Battle of Britain – stood up for what they believed in and were entirely on their own. They were the only ones to make a brave stand, managing to hold out against the abolition of slavery, proudly and unashamedly, with great dignity and nerve, hanging on to their slaves for as long as they possibly could, until, in the end, they had to bow to the inevitable – they had to give up their slaves and their institutionalised system of enslavement.

But why, we may ask, should a high proportion of Saudi Arabians *not* be in favour of slavery or, for that matter, institutionalised racism in their police force, army and so on? Why should they not? In view of their perfectly understandable history and their unenviable backwardness, why should these dinosaurs know any better? It's not their fault, poor things. They are merely the inevitable products of their history. They are not to blame.

As anyone knows who has travelled extensively in Saudi Arabia, the Saudi police are among the most racist in the world. It is an open secret. Many of their police take an obvious delight in questioning and arresting foreigners from all over the world, while Saudi Arabians look the other way and walk off, with or without a chuckle. Their police generally take the side of indigenous Saudis in any disputes, law-breaking or traffic accidents involving foreigners. If there is a choice between sending a Saudi law-breaker or an innocent foreigner to jail, the desert kingdom's police can usually be relied upon to point the finger of suspicion at the foreigners and put them behind bars.

There are plenty of innocent foreigners languishing behind bars in Saudi Arabia's rat-infested jails, crawling with cockroaches, and there is institutionalised torture as well as racism in these jails. Torture for the sake of torture, for the amusement of the Saudi police. But does the UN raise hell with the desert kingdom as a result? And does this prevent British royalty and other world leaders smiling sweetly in the direction of the Saudi royal family and its Government? Of course not.

Racism and torture were always a fact of life in the desert kingdom and both are still prevalent there today.

Not that Saudi Arabia's racism or slave trade prevented the high-profile world boxing champion, Mohammed Ali, from making his highly publicised pilgrimage to Mecca when he was in his prime, in the days when he was declaring the superiority of his religion, which he always claimed was anti-racist!

How ironic that he should have taken to a country that self-evidently believed that blacks were born to be slaves. How deeply sad and sadly ironic.

There was never any serious reason why observers should have been unduly surprised by the desert kingdom's refusal to abolish institutionalised slavery for such a long time. We are talking about a country that demanded the recall of British Ambassador (Sir Andrew Ryan) back in the early 1930s, because he involved himself in the freeing of a slave in the desert kingdom. This occurred under the terms of a 1927 independence treaty between Britain and its former protectorate, and thereby infuriated the father of the then Saudi foreign minister, whose slave the British Ambassador had helped to emancipate.

From the 1930s right through to the 1950s, the Saudi Arabians were turning a deaf ear to Britain's pleas for it to abolish slavery, and its sympathies were always closer to the white racists in South Africa and the deep South of the United States than ever they were to racial reformers and abolitionists for whom, traditionally, most Saudi rulers and royals have had little time, and to whom they have shown only contempt.

The founding king of Saudi Arabia is reputed to have had 42 sons who, between them, married an estimated 1,400 wives! With women being traded at the highest level, and sold into so-called matrimony at such a rate, can we really be surprised that the slavery of others for other purposes was regarded as such a small thing – the slavery of houseboys, servants, concubines, slave labourers and so on.

Saudi kings and royals have reportedly employed a network of scouts to comb the desert kingdom looking for new female talent to be purchased as wives and/or concubines, rather like European football managers employ scouts to look for soccer talent in Europe. And that female sexual talent has been bought and sold, like so much meat, with and without the consent of the women in question. It has been a great market of the flesh for the benefit of wealthy Arabs.

From the 1930s right through to the 1960s, Saudi rulers have either denied that institutionalised slavery existed in the desert kingdom, or they have told the outside world – when slavery could no longer be denied because the Saudis have been caught, as it were, red-handed – to mind its own business.

To this day, Saudi Arabians deny that there is an unofficial black market in slavery in the desert kingdom, where a closed market took over when the open market was finally closed down in the 1960s. They deny that there is no imported slave labour, that white and other foreign women are not being kidnapped and traded as slaves for the benefit of wealthy private individuals, harems and brothels tucked away in remote desert regions.

So tread with care in the desert kingdom.

Yes, there are pots of gold there, but when fools rush in, remember what can happen.

6

BLOOD MONEY

Blood money? Now there's a thought. It literally is what it suggests – money paid for the blood of a dead person, in return for spilling his or her blood, accidentally or otherwise, in return for taking someone's life, accidentally or otherwise.

Everything has a price, including life itself, however cheap that may be. If you kill or fatally injure someone, you can buy off their next-of-kin or relatives, and by so doing buy off the law of the land, if you shell out sufficient money to buy yourself a pardon.

Yes, in theory and not infrequently in practice, you can do that, unless the authorities have it in for you for some reason – in which case they may not let you off – or unless the next-of-kin or relatives of the person you have injured or killed are not inclined to be bought off.

So this blood money is a bit more than insurance. It is money for blood, other people's blood, should you kill or maim them in any type of accident, or in anger, through carelessness, or through deliberate acts of revenge, murder or anything that might cause harm in some way.

The money is calculated traditionally in terms of the market price of camels – and a man's life and blood is reckoned to be twice the value of a woman's.

But who can afford blood money? Not too many Bedouin or poor people unless the community comes to their aid with a whip-round – and certainly not all those impoverished foreigners, who work in the desert kingdom in order to enjoy inflated salaries and lower taxes. Many companies do not insure their employees against claims for blood money, so such employees are always at risk.

So that only leaves the rich, comfortably off or suitably insured, and there are a great many of the former in the desert kingdom.

Lorry and other drivers are not infrequently called upon to pay blood money in road accidents and, if they are found guilty, they are unceremoniously thrown into jail should they not be able to pay whatever sum of money is decided upon.

The thing about blood is that it is a lot easier to come by than paper money and coinage. People bleed easily, but they do not easily come by money, or part with it easily, for that matter. Money has to be earned and saved and bargained for. It can be stolen but not without effort – robbers have to break into banks, or pick pockets and raid retail outlets, while burglars have to break into houses. But to draw blood is effortless – the easiest thing in the world, accidentally or otherwise. It is a blank cheque. A scratch or a cut, a fall or collision will leak the red liquid in no time at all – and may result in a serious loss, including a loss of life if we are not careful.

Should such a loss result from an accident or deliberate act in which people are involved, then watch out in the desert kingdom, because someone will be crying foul and demanding blood money.

When there is bloodshed or a bloodbath, or when someone's blood is up, or there is bad blood between people, beware, because the words 'blood money' will instantly be uttered by the injured party, or the relatives and next-of-kin – and this will send your blood pressure soaring if you don't happen to have the money with which to pay up, or if you happen to be falsely accused and found guilty, simply because you have foreign blood.

And the thing about money is that, just like blood, you cannot do without it, even though you may not have much of it, either at all or when you most need it.

Of course, if you have married money, or made plenty of it, it won't bother you. Just as some people do not mind giving blood, because they feel that they have plenty to spare, you will not mind parting with your money.

And another thing about blood is that it's a precious gift, given to most of us in equal quantities and without prejudice, without regard to class or our station in life, and without regard to how hard we are prepared to work for it. It is our inheritance and birthright. We all inherit plenty of blood, but not too many of us inherit a great deal of money.

The desert kingdom's concept of, and insistence on, blood money makes you think about these things, not least when those who have a debt to pay can do so with camels instead of hard cash.

In relatively recent times, there was once a British Vice-Consul at the British Embassy in Jeddah, whose widow received £70,000 worth of blood money when a Saudi prince murdered her husband. The prince took a machete to the lowly diplomat and hacked him to death. There were all sorts of rumours about why he did this: he was drunk and was refused more whisky by the ill-fated diplomat when the prince attended a party in his house; he was having an affair with the diplomat's wife; he fancied the diplomat's wife and was angry that she remained faithful to her husband; he was drunk and didn't realise what he was doing ... The air was full of rumours for the simple reason that, instead of investigating such matters and reporting them openly, foreign governments and their diplomatic staff conspire with the Saudi authorities to hush such matters up.

The prince was drunk and didn't realise what he was doing? So how had he returned to the Vice-Consul's house with a machete, after he had left his house previously, without the obvious intention of harming him?

Perhaps he was angry and knew precisely what he was doing. Perhaps he felt insulted, humiliated and shamed to be refused more drink and turned out of the Vice-Consul's house in front of other guests. Perhaps, being a high-born prince of royal blood – one of the king's favourite sons, no less – he valued other people's blood and lives far less than his own. Perhaps he was mad with sexual jealousy. We shall never know the answers to any of these suggestions, because nobody bothered to investigate the matter, or if they did, they made damn sure not to let the public know about it. While the authorities and British Embassy could not deny that a Saudi prince had murdered a British diplomat, they could conceal and deny virtually everything else about this sordid and sorry affair.

While the prince was imprisoned for a few months – in the form of a comfortable house arrest – he was released after the murdered man's widow had been persuaded to accept blood money to the modest tune of £70,000 from the King of Saudi Arabia. A mere £70,000. It must have been the king's and the murderous prince's lucky day, the latter of whom was soon forgiven, just as his bloody crime was quickly forgotten. It's easy to forget things in a desert kingdom in which few records are kept of anything untoward or embarrassing, in which a cowed media is not allowed to publicise anything unflattering or unhelpful about the royal family.

Whilst the Saudi royal family and its Government is quick to execute others for murder, rape or adultery, it certainly doesn't expect to execute its own kind. Those of royal Saudi blood are in a favoured position when they commit the same crimes for which others would be executed.

But not only did the King and the royal family forgive this drunken prince for his crime, so, too, did the British Government and its Embassy in Jeddah, which took good care not to make waves as it drew a Saudi veil over its Vice-Consul's life, while discouraging the British media from investigating the matter further and refusing to co-operate with any press enquiries.

It is not clear who persuaded the dead man's widow to accept the derisory sum of £70,000 for the murder of her husband. The matter is too shrouded in mystery to know where the pressure came from, if indeed there was any pressure. Who is to say that the poor woman did not take the view that, since she had lost her husband, she might as well settle for £70,000, rather than demanding the Saudi prince's head and causing a big stink (a diplomatic incident that would have done irreparable harm to Saudi–British trade relations).

But what is crystal clear is that Brits and other foreign visitors in the desert kingdom of Saudi Arabia are not playing on a level playing field. They are, all of them – from the Government down to the lowliest worker – at an extreme disadvantage, and always will be for as long as the British Government and Foreign Office in London roll over every time the Saudis throw a tantrum (as it is to be hoped that they will not do when these true stories are published!) The Brits are not alone – Americans, Europeans and most others allow themselves to be pushed around in this way.

Maybe, next time the Saudi authorities lash British citizens or threaten to behead a Brit – as they do from time to time – the British ought to demand the head of the prince who murdered their diplomat.

7

THE COLOUR
IS WHITE

The desert is full of legends and mysteries, truths and half-truths, horrors and nightmares, myth and magic and sand! It is a bright, white empty canvas of gold and yellow and occasional black, with rare dashes of oasis green – painfully rare, and painfully green – in an otherwise grassless and lifeless wilderness. All of this is to be found under a blue-blue sky rapidly turning blackest-black at night and glittering magically with silvery garlands and necklaces of low-lying stars, sparkling, clear-as-daylight stars, as cool as ice in the inky blackness.

In such an empty place – that is nothing less than amazingly empty – there is not much drama around, apart from the drama of the unseen, which is by no means communicable to most people, let alone sensed or understood by them. But it is the kind of empty space that such dramatists as Beckett and

Pinter would die for, this extraordinary stage-set called the desert where, in the desert kingdom, one could and should stage such open-air theatre as would make world headlines, whilst bringing catharsis to where it is most needed.

This desert is a place of the unseen – unseen oil and unseen pipelines travelling underground, unseen people hanging out in unseen villages and oases, unseen warring tribesmen and unseen fates, unseen murders and rapes – all unspeakably unseen for most of the time, until, that is, somebody penetrates their mysteries and finds them at last, sees them at last, to record and report them at last, to write them into the sands of time for ever and a day. This desert is a place where anything and nothing happens right round the clock, at any time, regardless of time itself, in remote and unheard of places, miles and miles from anywhere.

People ride away into the desert – drive away into it – and disappear, never to be seen again. It swallows them up. Arabian fathers, shamed by their sexually permissive daughters, slit their throats and bury them in the desert in order to hide their shame. Arabian men, ashamed of themselves for succumbing to the sexual designs of foreign women – including the designs of Filipino and other nurses working in the desert kingdom – dispose of their perceived whores by strangling and burying them in the desert.

The desert swallows everything up and hides all disgrace out there in the great unseen. Even the sand itself can be unseen. One moment you are walking, or riding, or motoring on a great cushion or mattress of sand that is firm enough to support you, but the next moment some treacherous and unseen quicksand can swallow you up, sucking you into its depths, as you slip through its fingers while the sands of time run out for you at a rate of knots. The desert is such an unreliable and risky place, full of menacing uncertainty.

This is no place for people to live, but those who are not townsmen do live there just the same. It cannot be good for any of them. Those whose lot it is to live in among the hills and dunes of sand have come to resemble sand with their sandy weather-beaten faces, and their sand-swept hair and their sand-blasted hearts and souls. Like fog, sand confronts them everywhere. You cannot avoid it as you disappear into it and are swept along by it, sweeping and whirling sand, silently insinuating sand, sand creeping up on you from all directions, determining your unseen fate, more and more of it, is there no end to it?

So much sand, creeping into your sandals and clothes, into your hair and the creases of your skin as you battle with sandstorms, into your sand-caked eyes and mouth, into the air you breath, into your sensitive nostrils, into your heart and soul. You are positively drenched in sun and sand, swamped and blinded by sand, saturated by its overwhelming presence, swept along by oceans of it, tide after tide, for mile after mile, sinking into and disappearing behind clouds and mountains of sand – clogged and bogged down by it, shipwrecked and storm-tossed in it, utterly lost in it.

The desert kingdom is rooted and sinking in sand. Desert sand as an overwhelming metaphor for all that is wrong with desert lives is inescapable and obvious, monotonous and tedious. Its presence in the great unseen is everywhere in evidence, clearly visible to those who are prepared to peer beneath the surface.

The desert is also full of black shadows, tented shadows, and tented people whose desert mentality and history has come out of the shadows of their black tents, in stark contrast to the white and yellow sand that drives and connives against them.

But there are ominous white shadows, too – greater in number than the black shadows – which is why the colour is ultimately and overridingly white in the desert kingdom these days, as heart-stopping, pure white shadows suddenly come at you, out of the haunting landscape, into the foreground, and in the name of the king!

These are the dashing and fearsome White Guard – the ferocious king's men – who suddenly pop up like devilish genii from nowhere. These ghostly white warriors draw nearer and nearer, galloping at speed, camel-riding at speed, armoured-vehicles motoring at speed, tumbling out of helicopters at speed. Out of a misty heat haze they come, like a quivering bright light, out of the desert sun, sometimes with their swords shining, other times with their gun barrels gleaming.

That's what the desert provides for you more than anything else – sublime mental confusion and, to prove it, here come the king's personal bodyguards, to keep the desert pristine white, striking at will in remote places, wherever and whenever there is opposition to their puritanical flame, or whenever there is a threat to national security. Their reputation has gone before them for decades, these cut-throat fiends in white, who think nothing of cutting a man to pieces, or spiking his head as a warning to others. They come out of the black shadows of night, out of the black daytime shadows of distant tents and camel trains, out of the great unknown.

It is estimated that there are at least 32,000 of these whiter-than-white devils from Bedouin rank and file, and from the fanatical rank and file of Wahhabi tribesmen. They are all religious zealots, each and every one of them, predictably loyal to their desert king and keeping faith with their religious belief, ever ready to draw blood and to kill as they continue their moral crusade for a supposedly puritanical and Arab way of life.

This legendary White Guard – with its blood-and-guts reputation for brutality and barbarism – haunts the desert, day and night. It is separated out from the 25,000-strong Army, which is recruited from desert townsmen with whom the king and his royal family are reputedly out of sympathy. And why wouldn't they be, since it is the townsmen from which a new and more liberal-minded class will come. If it is to come at all, it will be from its academics, social reformers, democrats, journalists, school teachers and modern-minded soldiers, airmen and seamen – which, perish the thought, is neither intended nor wished for by the King and his White Guard. Separate from the Army, the White Guard is kept better armed and equipped than the lesser fighting force that is recruited (and downgraded) from populated areas and then hidden away behind sand dunes, out in the desert (while the regulars of the White Guard stay in the towns and cities, close to the royal family, for ceremonial and security purposes, but can strike like lightning by air or land, whenever and wherever they may be needed in unseen desert backwaters, in the remote places far removed from the seats of power). Overnight, or in the afternoons, these city-based white ghosts can suddenly penetrate deep into the desert, wreaking havoc wherever they go, turning sweet sleep into the stuff of nightmares.

There is, in the desert kingdom, nowhere beyond their elongated white grasp, and there is no place that is safe from them, as they come out of the white-hot heat, with a bloodstained grin on their ferocious faces, white as ghosts in their aggressively white and flowing uniforms.

Apart from the desert kingdom's air force – at least 70 per cent of whose pilots and others are reckoned to be royalists through and through – they are the determining factor in the home-front military, these men who are supposed to be the hand of God and the King in the desert kingdom, complete with their tanks and other modern weapons of war that make horses and camels redundant.

And there is much work for this White Guard to do. From the 1950s right through to the '80s and '90s, there have been unpublicised rebellions and uprisings for them to put down, and some publicised ones as well, including the 1979 uprising in Mecca when some 300 religious fanatics occupied the Grand Mosque in that holiest of holy Muslim cities, and not even the White Guard could solve the problem. Which is why, presumably, the King and his Government called upon French paratroopers from the Christian world and gave them special dispensation to enter the holy city and smoke the fanatics out, after which 63 of the prisoners were taken on a road show around the desert kingdom, paraded in the streets and publicly executed – beheaded – for all to see, televising each execution so that Arabian people in their homes could also be reminded that uprisings will not be tolerated.

The word is that the French paratroopers flooded the mosque and then connected an electricity supply to the water, flooding, shocking and electrocuting the rebels out. The word is that the much admired and feared White Guard still has a lot to learn.

As an exclusively Bedouin and Wahhabi tribal force, officers and soldiers of the White Guard swear a personal allegiance to their king before their country, and their chief purpose is to protect the royal family. They are not unlike the Brigade of Guards in England, in as much as their officers have to come from the same élite tribal class or background in order to get into the Guard, and they have to put their monarch before and above their country. And they must go about their duties with a fanatical intensity!

That the desert kingdom's royal family owes much to the White Guard and the ugly tribal communities from which it was initially drawn is not in doubt. It was Bedouin and fanatical Wahhabi sheikhs who had not only toiled for years to help put the founding king on the throne, back in 1927, but also helped to keep him there. And they put him on the throne having been supplied with British arms.

In the service of the founding king, they gleefully and proudly announced that they took no prisoners, as they spiked the heads of their enemies and displayed them on the gates of the cities that fell to them, while also taking the greatest care to burn their prisoners to death for their own amusement, before gang-raping women and then slave-trading them and selling or gifting them to their friends and acquaintances, all in the proud name of their 'superior' religion. All this and more they did in the name of their savage puritanical and royal fervour, which elevated them above lesser mortals. Self-righteous, hypocritical, outrageously prejudiced and nonsensical, the desert kingdom's Wahhabis and Bedouin were all these things when they brought the founding king to his throne. Their backers – the British – turned a blind eye and took good care not to write about this in the travel books and diaries of the White Arabs who enthused so romantically about them, after Britain had put its puppet king on his throne.

And out of such a disgraceful, starchy-white womb was born this legendary White Guard. And it is these pampered and self-righteous people who are putting the frighteners on other more liberal-minded and civilised Muslims in the desert kingdom today, who are keeping the desert puritanical white, as white as the driven snow, which never falls in the hot and arid land of the pure.

So the desert is white – in more ways than one – and for as long as the White Guard are prepared to fight, it is likely to remain that way.

8

THE TRAVELLER HAS
HIS OWN EXCUSES

The desert – being remote, inaccessible and endlessly distant – is a good place in which to hide from the outside world, in amongst the giant waves of sand in which one can be lost at sea forever.

Many visitors have perished there, whilst others have gone into the desert to find themselves, to be at one with nature and to keep their own company, in the wall-to-wall silence that is laid like a carpet from end to end. Some people have gone there to think, and to avoid the spontaneity of the outside world, in the emptiest and most silent place in the world, a back-of-beyond place that has gone into its shell, like a tortoise. Such people go into their shells, likewise, and it is anybody's guess what is going on when a tortoise goes into its shell, or what may happen when it comes out of it.

There are those who go into the desert to study the scriptures and practise their race hate, before returning to Britain and other parts of Europe where they preach it, as in the case of the Muslim cleric in London who was tried and convicted of three counts of soliciting murder, after he told young Muslims in the UK to 'fly planes, drive tanks, use guns and missiles' in a holy war against 'non-believers', and for which he promised rewards in heaven that included 72 virgins! Oh yes, this too is taught in desert communities.

Writers who are intensely private and deliberately inaccessible may go into the desert to commune, not only with nature, but also with themselves, from head to toe. They may not go there for their readers at all and, being intensely private, they may not write anything nakedly revealing about their experiences. They may prefer to project a persona, like a character in an opera who neither speaks nor sings, or like a diplomat who is *persona grata* to a fault. They may be so determined to avoid spontaneity and directness in their writing that they draw a mysterious veil over their words in order to intrigue and become subtle, in which case it is to be hoped that what is going on behind the veil – that the writer behind the mask – is genuinely subtle and intriguing, otherwise we are left with boredom and emptiness, which is what we find in the desert most of the time.

Of course, different people feel differently about the desert and their own infinitesimal place in it, and some people feel nothing at all because they are overwhelmed by nothingness, and may have gone there in order to feel and become nothing at all, not even a blot or a spot on the distant landscape. They are out of their minds with nothing at all, and the failure of imagination to which this gives rise.

But there are also writers who cannot afford such

unimaginative luxuries. Because they are stricken by an incurable writing bug, they must write about how they feel, and some will write naturally about their own genuine feelings, whilst others will keep their feelings out of it, and others again may do their best to *will* their readers to feel things that they might not have felt otherwise (some may alternate between each of these things). If they are to use a persona at all, writers must ask themselves some searching questions about the reasons why and precise nature of its use, and if they are to deliver their copy on time, they had better not get lost in the desert for too long. Whilst paper is patient and the Arabs are the first to concede that 'the desert traveller has his own excuses' – for arriving late or not at all – readers have other things on their minds if a writer doesn't get a move on and show up when he is expected to do so.

But the problem for all writers, when putting pen to paper, is how to give voice to the silent scream that is the desert's only story?

The traveller may have his own excuses, but there is no excuse for not writing about this.

9

HOLY AIR AND
SACRED SKIES

The desert kingdom is under the impression that the heaven-sent air in the skies over the holy city of Mecca is blessed by the Almighty in the land of the pure.

For this reason, it will not allow non-Muslim pilots to fly their aeroplanes through this precious Mecca air that is breathing God's will into the holiest of all cities, the skies of which are reckoned to be truly sacred. It is figured that non-Muslims flying through the sacred skies above Mecca would contaminate the hot air like a moral stain up there in the heavens.

While a special dispensation was granted to French paratroopers to enter the city of Mecca when the terrorists took over the Grand Mosque there, and the desert kingdom's Army and White Guard couldn't flush them out, that was a one-off, previously unheard of, not to be repeated again.

The desert kingdom has, in its time, forced insect-spraying aircraft from the Swiss company, Ciba Geigy to remove its famous Christian cross from the sides of its aeroplanes when flying low over Mecca to kill off mosquitoes and other pests. It has also insisted that the company, along with all airlines flying over Mecca, should use Muslim (chiefly Pakistani) pilots.

On the ground, there is even a 'heathen's highway' to enforce non-Muslims to bypass Mecca in their cars and lorries, rather than go anywhere near the holy city, from which they must be kept at arm's length.

Perhaps we should not be surprised by this in a country that will not allow non-Muslims living in the community either to say their prayers in public places or to keep or wear religious symbols, because this is supposed to be offensive to Muslims. Outside the compounds of foreign embassies from the Christian world, Christian churches and places of worship are strictly forbidden.

When I entered the desert kingdom, it was necessary for me to carry a reference from a Christian vicar or priest, in the form of a Certificate of the Christian Religion, stapled into my passport to prove that I was not a hated Jew or an atheist, who were public enemies number one and two. And I flew straight into Jeddah, well clear of Mecca's sacred skies.

Being an agnostic and/or atheist – depending on the circumstances and my mood – it was difficult for me to get the necessary Certificate of Religion because I had not been to church for such a long time. So I went to my former church, the beautiful St Bart's, in Cloth Fair in the City of London, where the vicar had not seen me for more than a decade, and I asked him if he could oblige me with a short note saying that I was a practising Christian.

As you might expect, he couldn't remember me at first, but when the penny finally dropped, he said, 'Now I remember you – you're that atheist chappie who used to argue with me about religion.'

'Yes, that's exactly who I am,' I replied. 'Which is why I have come to see you, because I do not know any other vicars. Yours is the only church I have been to in many a year now. I have attended some services here, with your old friend and member of congregation, Lesley Jervis, who was always a devout Christian, of course, and I have arranged for my good friend, Tony Wardle, to marry here. I also remember organising Jervis's memorial service, with Baroness von Neurat here, after Jervis snuffed it in Somerset, and when the baroness's suitor, Professor Catlin, gave the service.'

'But why should I write a reference for you when you are not a good practising Christian?' the vicar asked. 'Why should I write a reference for somebody who always claimed to be an atheist.'

I thought about this for a short while before replying, 'Because I am a Christian atheist, so you have some small responsibility for me.'

He smiled to himself before looking up at me with a puzzled expression, 'Why did you say that you needed such a certificate?'

'Because I am going to the desert kingdom of Saudi Arabia and the Saudi Government will not admit me without a certificate on the letterhead of a Christian church that has to be stapled into my passport.'

'Well I never,' he said, 'what a funny world we live in. Are you seriously telling me that these bloody heathens will not let a Christian into their country without proof of his religion, whilst they come and go with impunity here in London all the time?'

'Exactly,' I replied.

'I'll tell you what,' he said, 'pop into the pub next door and order me a double gin and tonic, while I scribble you a note to the effect that you are a regular church-goer. I don't suppose God will mind my telling a white lie to heathens of all people. The pub's called the Hand and Shears. I don't know if you remember it?'

'Oh yes, I remember it well,' I told him 'and I particularly remember its delicious potato salad, full of garlic and chopped onions. It used to be run by a retired officer in the Hungarian Army, with a splendid curly moustache, aided by his wife. I also remember the timbered house of Sir John Betjeman, the poet, just across the road from your church.'

'That's right, it's still there,' he replied, 'now go and get the drinks in while I behave like a British Ambassador and lie for my country.'

Ambassadors are, of course, men who go out into the world to lie for their countries, even the most religious of them, and not least Saudi Arabian ambassadors. I thought about this as I made my way to the Hand and Shears where I ordered two large gins, complete with tonic water, ice and lemon.

This was how I came by a Certificate of the Christian Religion, without which I could not get into the desert kingdom of Saudi Arabia.

But my story doesn't end here.

Over a couple of gins and tonics in the pub over the road from the church, my new Certificate of the Christian Religion was signed, and I was ready for the trip into the unknown.

After my first three months in the desert kingdom, where I was on a visitor's visa, I was required to apply for a proper work permit and, to do this, I had to exit the country for the sake of

Saudi law, and go to the nearest Saudi Arabian Embassy overseas to apply for a work permit on foreign soil, before re-entering the desert kingdom. So I went to Cairo, where the Saudi Embassy told me to come back in ten days, since it could not be expected to process the permit any quicker.

After ten days' holiday in Cairo, I went back to the Embassy, picked up my passport, which had a work permit stamped into it, written and signed in Arabic, so I could not read what it said.

I then flew back to Jeddah where a Saudi Arabian colleague took one look at the permit stamped in my passport and declared, 'Good God! They've made a mistake. They've written Muslim in Arabic where there is a question about your religion. They've turned you into one of us, my friend. You are a Muslim now. Welcome to Islam.'

So, in a little more than three months, I had graduated from atheism to Christianity to Islam. Not bad progress for an unbeliever! All I needed now was to become a Jew and perhaps a Hindu as well, and I would be assured of a place in any of the heavenly kingdoms, up there with the gods, which is more than most people can say.

I said to my Saudi Arabian colleague, 'Perhaps we can go to Mecca one day, you and I?'

'I wouldn't risk it, if I were you,' he replied, 'because if they started to ask you questions about the Muslim religion, you wouldn't have a clue, so they would soon find you out, and punish you accordingly. Better steer clear of Mecca, you bloody heathen.'

And steer clear of Mecca I did, under its sacred skies and holy air.

10

IT STANDS TO
REASON

Farida is a beautiful and glamorous young Arabian woman. Her breathtaking beauty is of Ava Gardner or Sophia Loren proportions. She has more than enough beauty for one woman. Because she likes being beautiful, she revels in it, and knows how to flaunt it. But much good may it do her in the desert kingdom, where the fact is that such women are kept hidden away behind the shape-obscuring *burka*.

Her face is bursting to be seen, but like other Arabian women, she must hide it behind a veil and walk respectfully behind the men in her life. Her curvaceous and ample body is likewise crying out to be seen, but it cannot be revealed to anyone other than herself. She makes her face up with the most expensive Western cosmetics, and she wears the flimsiest of veils in the hope that her flashing eyes and stunning smile might be appreciated by the opposite sex with whom she naturally wants to share her beauty. Her luscious lips are pouting and beautifully made up and her eyes are framed with the best eyeliners. She is glamorous indeed, behind the veil.

Being female, she is not allowed to drive a car, like her male counterparts, or to have a career of her own. Because Arabian women are not allowed into the desert kingdom's workplace, she can only imagine what it is like to have a job. Coming from a rich family, Farida is not in need of a salary, but she does want a job and the social life that goes with it. She wants to get on with her life. And she wants to get out of her parents' stifling and claustrophobic house during the day and use her brain. She hates vegetating, as most women do in the desert kingdom, and she cannot wait to blossom and flower. She wants a man, of course, a handsome and intelligent man who has been educated at university (as has she, in Cairo, after finishing school in Europe). She wants to be able to choose her own man. But, as a contemporary of the high-ranking princess who was so cruelly executed in public by her wicked grandfather – for taking a young man against her parents' wishes – Farida suspects that this is not possible, not really. She must wait for her parents to find a suitable young man for her, with wealth and the right family background, and she must give up any foolish notions of a career in the desert kingdom.

She knows that, apart from foreign nurses, nannies, school teachers, air hostesses and the occasional office secretary, there are few working women in the desert kingdom, even though some have recently been admitted as undergraduates to local universities. She also knows that the workplace is forbidden to virtually all Arabian women, and this makes her angry. She is impatient for social change, but it does not come, and this frustrates her much more than it frustrates other women who were not sent abroad for their education, so are used to staying at home and occupying their thoughts with nothing more than domestic matters.

Feeling that her education is wasted on her, Farida is angry about this as well. Why send her abroad to use her brain, and then bring her home to neglect it and let it rust?

But for a frustrated and restless woman – angry, too, with the desert kingdom's men, who subjugate their womenfolk – Farida manages to remain good-natured most of the time. Her anger is mild and short-lived, with a petulance that is not vindictive and does not harbour grudges. And, having a good sense of humour, she can generally see the funny side of most things, not least her own anger. But she does have a short fuse when irritated by men who say stupid things about women.

Farida doesn't go to the beach. This is because it is a segregated all-female beach, forbidden to men, who similarly have segregated beaches of their own. The reason why Farida doesn't go to the female beach is because women must swim fully dressed there for fear of being spied on by the opposite sex who might otherwise catch a distant glimpse of them in their bikinis, if they were allowed to wear them, which they are not. Perish the thought! Bikini-clad Arabian women for men to feast their eyes on, as they do when they go to the West. What a depraved idea.

There is another reason why Farida doesn't go to the all-female beach. In the absence of men, frustrated and sex-starved women become so hungry for it, so desperate for sexual comfort and relief, that they develop lesbian tendencies towards other women, inviting them back to their houses for all-female parties and dances (supervised by their mothers and grandmothers), and pestering heterosexual women to indulge in a lesbian affair until such time as they can have and marry a man. The same thing happens on the all-male beaches, where men strike up sexual relationships with other men because they cannot get access to women. These homosexual and lesbian relationships are conducted discreetly, behind locked doors, but they are negotiated on the segregated beaches. Because the idea of a lesbian relationship makes Farida's flesh creep, because it accentuates the dreadful feelings of waste and desolation that she is already undergoing, she steers clear of these depressing beaches.

She also steers clear of sexually segregated cinemas, in which single women sit in the dark on one side of a wall running down the centre of the auditorium, dividing them from single men who sit on the other side, and she hardly ever visits ice cream parlours where young men and women sit at separate tables, a safe distance from one another, because they are forbidden to have any social intercourse. Only married couples are allowed to sit together in cinemas and ice-cream parlours, providing they are sporting their wedding rings to prove that they are married.

As for sexually segregated buses, Farida never has to take one, thanks to her family owning a chauffeur-driven car that is generally at her disposal. But Farida does go to a women's bank to collect the weekly allowance that her generous and doting father deposits there for her.

With common consent, the desert kingdom is a place like no other. It has been said before and will doubtless be said again. Everybody says so, everybody knows it, and few, hand on heart, are particularly proud of it. But, being an incurably proud people – scared to death by the possibility of shame, or dishonour, and not given to social change – those who live there must pretend that things are as they should be.

Farida has had more than enough of the desert kingdom, the place of her birth and early education, the place where she must now accustom herself to spending the rest of her life, married or otherwise.

Her father is a good and kindly man, who loves his daughter dearly, and he has educated her abroad where she has perfected her English and studied subjects denied to schoolgirls and women in the desert kingdom. Having schooled her in Saudi Arabia to begin with, he has also sent her to an English-language school in Cairo, a finishing school in Switzerland and university back in Cairo again. So Farida has seen something of the outside world and she has enjoyed every minute of it. She has holidayed in London, Paris and Rome, and developed a strong taste for the outside world that is not yet satisfied. But her father hopes for a time when women will be liberated in his country, and he is looking for a handsome young suitor for his daughter, of whom he can approve. While his daughter is not in a hurry to marry, she does crave the company of men.

One day he tells his daughter that he has bumped into an old friend who is launching an English-language newspaper.

'How exciting,' says Farida, 'how I should love to be a journalist, with my own column in a newspaper, to write what I like and encourage readers, especially stay-at-home women, to write to me, as they do in Western papers.'

Her father smiles his indulgent, paternal smile, but shakes his head. 'Not in this country, my sweet one. No newspaper columns by Arabian female journalists here, I'm afraid. Not in my lifetime, at any rate.'

Farida is appalled to hear this, but she is nothing if not optimistic. 'Don't be such a pessimist, father. Not in your lifetime, indeed. You have such a long time to live yet, so there is plenty of time for things to change for young women in this country. Future generations of women cannot stay at home for ever. It could happen one of these days – in the not too distant future – that you will be reading a column in a Saudi newspaper by an Arabian woman. By your daughter perhaps. Why not? You should suggest it to Jalal when you next see him. He is exactly the sort to give it a try.'

Jalal is the founding editor of the daily newspaper in question and, as Farida rightly observes, he is exactly the sort to give it a try. Upon his return from university in the USA, he signed a petition for the liberation of women in the desert kingdom – and, in particular, for their release from *purdah* – for which he was immediately put under house arrest and interrogated for a week, just to remind him that he was back home again, where such outrageous ideas were not welcome. Had he not been the son of a respected holy man, he would certainly have been thrown into a rat-infested prison cell, crawling with ants and cockroaches, but as a privileged member of the upper classes, he was let off lightly with a house arrest. Yes, Farida is right, he is *exactly* the man to push back the boundaries, by publishing a newspaper column by an Arabian female journalist, to see if he and she can get away with it. With Jalal's help, the ambitious Farida could easily become the kingdom's first female journalist. He is liberal-minded, unafraid of the authorities – whom he regards as a joke most of the time – and his family is sufficiently influential and well connected to hold its own and keep him out of trouble should things go wrong, as long as he doesn't go too far. Providing the desert kingdom with its first female journalist could not be described as going too far, could it? It might be frowned upon to begin with, but people would get used to it, and before long there would be quite a number of Arabian women in the kingdom taking to journalism like ducks to water. Of course, female journalists couldn't go out on to the streets, into the world of men, and interview people there, but surely they could sit sedately behind their desks, keeping their cute noses out of men's affairs, and writing newspaper columns for other women?

'Oh, do suggest it to him, father,' Farida continues. 'If he won't give it a try, I don't know who else will in this country. Most men are such wimps here. Tell him that I would love to write a column for him. What harm could come of it? At worst, the government might make him withdraw the column. But it's not going to execute anybody for such a thing. And who knows? If Jalal tries it, with his popularity in high places, the government and royal family might just be in the mood to go along with it. Several of his friends are in the government and he has plenty of money to buy himself out of trouble, or to bribe others if that's what it takes. If they catch the King in a good mood one day, it might just work.'

Farida's father takes a deep breath. 'And if the King wakes up in a bad mood one day, he might just have the column withdrawn! It's a good idea, I grant you. But I'm not sure about the government. Whilst it might not execute my precious daughter for writing a newspaper column under her own name, it might put her under house arrest. And who knows? On a bad day, the government might get it into its head to give Jalal a public flogging for daring to publish her column in his newspaper. You think Jalal and his family would thank us for that?'

Farida is not only optimistic, she is tempestuous with it. 'I should think that Jalal would be proud to be flogged for such a worthy cause, brave man that he is. As for me, I don't give a damn for their house arrests. Let them arrest me, if they want to make fools of themselves.'

Her father rolls his eyes and sighs. 'Don't be ridiculous, Farida. Like any man, brave or otherwise, Jalal would not be amused to be flogged, and his family might very well blame us for his predicament. As for my daughter being put under house arrest, I couldn't bear it, so I won't hear of her risking it. Please don't mention this matter again. A newspaper column for you – or any other women in the kingdom – is out of the question at this point in our history. It stands to reason that the Royal Family would not allow it, and as for the government, I'm not sure that they would favour it either.'

But Farida is not finished yet. 'Nothing in this unreasonable country, father, can ever possibly "stand to reason". There *is* no reason here. It is the most unreasonable place in the world. The government would favour it if they heard that the King favoured it. It's as simple and unreasonable as that.'

Farida's father is becoming exasperated with his daughter. 'But how on earth would the government hear such an extremely unlikely thing from the king? What reason would it have to hear it from him, of all people, and what reason would he have to favour such a thing? He hasn't taken leave of his senses, has he? He hasn't become a modern man, a man of reason! Really, Farida, get real, as you young people say. Join the real world. This is the desert kingdom you are talking about, not your enlightened European countries. This is a place where women must never forget their place. I sometimes think that I should never have sent you abroad for your education. Maybe you would have been more content if I had kept you at home and had you educated here. As for this country being a stranger to reason, it has a backward logic and reason all its own and, believe me, I have studied it, and I know how it works, unlike reasonable people elsewhere.'

End of discussion.

One day, when she is alone in the house, Farida summons the family chauffeur to take her into town. She instructs him to drive her into the docks and wait for her outside a dilapidated old office building, through the corridors of which she breezes like a breath of fresh air – like a bird in full flight as she carries all before her – with her veil pulled tightly across her face.

'Where's Jalal's office?' she asks a startled young Arabian man.

'At the end of this corridor,' he replies.

Bursting in, uninvited, Farida drops her veil in Jalal's office, entrancing him with her infectious smile as he sits behind his desk, looking up at her in utter amazement.

He is predictably amazed to see her standing there, so unexpected and unannounced, but he is quickly and completely under her spell. 'Farida, what a lovely surprise. You are as beautiful as ever, I see. But what are you doing here? Is your father with you?'

'I want to talk to you,' says Farida, closing the door behind her.

Jumping up from his desk at once, Jalal rushes to the door and opens it again. 'Men are not allowed to have female visitors in their offices with their doors closed, Farida. The religious police forbid it. So doors must remain open at all times when men and women find themselves in the same room.'

'How ridiculous,' Farida responds. 'What a very stupid country this is. Religious police indeed. Who needs them? What's it to dirty old men like them?'

Jalal grins a large grin, as he returns to his desk, seating himself opposite Farida on the far side. 'Shsssh, please, Farida. Keep your voice down. People may hear us through the open door. Any one of my staff may be on his way out of the building, as we speak, to find a religious policeman and report to him that I have a woman in my office.'

Farida remains unimpressed. 'The religious police can go fuck themselves, for all I care. They are the lowest of the low. I hate them.'

'Yes, yes, Farida,' says Jalal lowering his voice, 'but *do please keep your voice down* – people are listening.'

'That's because the door is wide open,' she replies, 'we need to shut it if I am to tell you what I have come to say.'

Jalal gets up from behind his desk again and whispers: 'Follow me.'

The two of them disappear down the corridor and into a lift which takes them up to a flat roof. Jalal asks her, 'Now then, what is it you have come to say, my beauty? No one can hear us up here on the roof.'

'But it's too damn hot,' says Farida, 'there's no shelter from the sun up here.'

Jalal shrugs. 'Best I can do, I'm afraid.'

When Farida has finished explaining to Jalal the kind of newspaper column that she wants to write for his newspaper, he is overjoyed at the prospect: 'What a brilliant idea. Why didn't I think of it myself?'

'Because you're a man?' she suggests.

Jalal is all for it and he tells Farida, 'This is the best idea I've heard all week and I'd love you to write a column for me. But first I must clear it with the Minister of Information, who is a good friend of mine, and see if he cannot get it past the king, to whom he is related. The Oil Minister is very close to the king, of course, and he is an excellent friend, so I shall consult him also, to see if he cannot have a word in the royal ear. There are also some other members of the ruling classes who are enlightened enough to play ball. I was at the home of one of them up in the mountains last weekend, at a farewell party for his younger daughter, before she left for Cambridge, where she was playing a guitar and singing Western pop songs to invited guests – *and* wearing a low-cut dress with a deliciously plunging neckline, I am glad to say.'

'While a young schoolgirl, round the corner in the same village, was expelled from school by the Director of Religious Education, and then ostracised by the entire community merely for saying, in an Arabic magazine, that she loved an Arabian musician!' says Farida with a look of disgust on her face. 'The authorities think nothing of falsely accusing a village girl who happens to be a nobody, but they wouldn't dare try it on with the Oil Minister's daughters, who are, of course, somebody special.'

'So you heard about that, too,' Jalal replies, 'it is awful, isn't it? I share your disgust, Farida. I hear that they will not allow the girl back into school. She is being treated as if she were no better than a whore. What a sad, sick joke this country of ours is. Let's hope we can change things before long. But not in your column, mind you. We cannot risk anything too controversial, political or religious, I'm afraid. You'll have to keep it very homespun and folksy.'

Farida sighs a heavy sigh and pulls a face. 'Yes, I realise that. But how long do you think it will take for you to get approval? And will you go ahead without approval, if necessary?'

Jalal tells her that, if the Oil Minister sounds the king out successfully, as he may do, then it would be better to wait for royal approval. If not, he will go ahead without it, but not before warning the Minister of Information, so that he can prepare himself with a ready argument should he need to keep the critics at bay and defend the newspaper in the event of flak.

He also tells her that he must fly to London and Bombay to recruit some British and Indian journalists, so he will be away for a couple of weeks.

But she is not impressed. 'Why do women always have to wait in this damn country? Wait on men, wait on the centuries-old prejudice against women. It's too much!'

Jalal bursts out laughing, 'Oh, Farida, what a breath of fresh air you are. I could kiss you for your impertinence and admirable disrespect.'

Farida's mouth falls open at the prospect. 'Kiss me? You'd better not. You're a man – and a married man at that.'

'Quite so,' says Jalal. 'I'd better not, and it was said jokingly. I think! So don't worry.'

Farida walks straight up to Jalal, who is a good-looking man, and she holds her face close to his. 'It doesn't *worry* me, Jalal. It's you and your wife I am thinking of.'

Whereupon she turns on her heel and walks across the roof and back into the lift, with Jalal quickly following her. After she has thanked him for his time and left the building, Jalal returns to his office and immediately gets on the phone to the Minister of Information and the Oil Minister, both of whom share his enthusiasm for Farida's 'harmless' and perfectly charming idea. Jalal then picks up the phone to ring Farida on her return to her parents' house, telling her that she has their support also, and she is, of course, delighted. How can her father possibly disagree now?

'Jalal,' she says, before she puts down the phone, 'I'm beginning to think that, figuratively speaking, I could kiss you, too.'

Soon, Jalal's daily newspaper is up and running, and journalists from London are urinating on the roof of the building where Jalal has had his historic rendezvous with Farida. The reason for this is that the faulty and overflowing toilets in the dilapidated newspaper offices are so disgusting – with excreta floating in the urine that spills over the floor – that the journalists cannot bring themselves to use them. So they sneak up to the roof instead, for a quick pee in the blinding sun, which is so hot that the roof is quickly cleansed of its urine (meanwhile, on surrounding rooftops, giggling Arabian women, young and old, peep through their washing lines for a glimpse of the journalists' exposed private parts).

Because there are too many power strikes, journalists on night shift accustom themselves to working by candlelight, as well as to rats roaming into their offices and rummaging around in the discarded bits of paper under their desks and in their waste paper baskets. Sometimes they chase these rats out of their offices, at other times they are too busy, so they just ignore them. Some journalists find the heat and the culture clash too much, so they return home in a matter of weeks. Those who survive three months pass the acid test, and stay much longer – sometimes for years.

To begin with, Jalal has some problems with the distribution of his newspaper when the Arabian delivery boys – who are paid to get the publication to its subscribers, including the foreign embassies in addition to the bookstalls – take the view that it is easier to go into the desert and throw the paper away, rather than tracking down so many different private addresses in an anonymous kingdom in which most of the streets are without names, just as the high-walled private villas and the office buildings are without numbers. Losing patience with such vague instructions as 'third or fourth house on the right, in the fifth street that is behind that road that is pointed in the direction of nowhere special, but is frequented by foreign workers these days ...' they elect to get shot of the newspapers in the desert and hope that no one notices. But, eventually, Jalal manages to solve his delivery problem, as paid subscribers complain that they have not received their copies, and deductions are made to the delivery boys' pay packets whenever complaints are received.

Taxi drivers in the desert kingdom have the same problem as the newspaper delivery boys when it comes to identifying streets and knowing where they are supposed to be going. As former Bedouin peasants who have never driven a car in their lives – and have not been required to pass much of a driving test in order to get a licence – they are lost in towns and cities with streets with no names, as they drive their vehicles recklessly, like lunatics, almost beating them as they would a camel, to make them go faster. With one foot nailed to the throttle, they are not good at braking as and when required, and their impatience is such that, when the road ahead is congested, they either bump and hoot the car in front, urging it to get out of their way, or they simply take to the pavements instead, putting the fear of God into pedestrians as well as their passengers. Any unaccompanied non-Arabian woman who is foolish enough to take one of these cabs could be taken into the desert and raped and abandoned there by the drivers. It has happened before. Foreign workers and visitors from the Third World must also accustom themselves to having their faces customarily slapped, should it transpire, when they are asked outright, that they do not share the driver's religion. Taking to the roads in a car in the desert kingdom is like participating in a wartime invasion, storming the beach-heads and turning this way and that to avoid instant death, as one weaves in and out of other vehicles, some of which think nothing of going down one-way streets the wrong way, against the advancing traffic!

It is against this nightmarish background that Jalal clearly has his hands full, launching his daily newspaper, getting it delivered and his staff to their appointments on time and in one piece.

Meanwhile, Farida sits and waits, hoping for news from Jalal. She has told her father of her visit to him in his office and she has convinced him that no harm can come of it. He, too, has spoken to Jalal, who has reassured him, so he is no longer worried, this man who loves his daughter dearly, and is now beginning to feel quietly proud of her. What a girl she is! A column in a desert kingdom newspaper, no less. The country's first female journalist.

'What a pity,' Farida remarks, 'that Arabian women are not allowed to have their faces photographed in the desert kingdom. Otherwise, I might have my photograph at the top of my column.'

But her father cautions her, 'Don't think of showing your face to the masses yet, my sweet one. Your name alone will cause quite a stir.'

After kissing her father on both cheeks, Farida takes leave of him and goes off to see her mother, who is equally proud of her daughter, but none the less worried about what people might think and say when they read her column. But Farida tells her, 'Don't worry, Mummy, with the Minister of Information approving every word that I write and signing off on it, I hardly think that anybody is going to take offence – except me!'

Farida is quite a girl and, when a nod and wink comes through from the royal palace to Jalal, signalling that he can give Farida's column a try, she is elated.

She tells Jalal, 'You don't have to pay me for it, you know. I don't need the money. That's not why I am doing it.'

'Of course you're not doing it for the money,' he replies, 'but we shall pay you just the same, and handsomely, too, for I have some wealthy backers – oil sheikh millionaires – until such time as we get the government grant. You know the type.'

'Oh yes, I know the type,' she replies, shaking her head disapprovingly.

Jalal looks at her quizzically. 'Tell me, Farida, how do you find this kingdom, after your absence abroad?'

A serious expression descends like a cloud on Farida's beautiful face. 'Don't ask, Jalal, you don't want to know.'

'But I do,' he persists.

There is a studied pause, and then she tells him. 'OK, here's what I think, if you really want to know. To me, this kingdom is a puppet show. *Punch and Judy* in the sand. Strings are being pulled under the sand in the form of pipelines – oil pipelines, the invisible and tacky strings of which connect to a mysterious outside world, Jalal, where only a privileged few from the desert kingdom can afford to go. But internally, within the kingdom, nothing ever connects, other than these pesky pipelines, hidden from view, under the sand. Men and women do not connect; there is no connection of body and soul; truth and justice do not connect; freedom and democracy do not connect; and mercy and compassion – those two cornerstones of all morality – do not connect. Time itself does not connect, either from hour to hour, day to day, or month to month. With so little for most people to do, and next to nothing going on, time is almost irrelevant. In the desert, the traveller has his own excuses. He may or may not turn up to keep an appointment with you today, tomorrow, or sometimes never. He does not connect with the ticking of a clock, or indeed with any causal logic in a desert kingdom in which two and two might just as well make five, and it frequently does so.

'Our nameless and unidentified roads, and our numberless and anonymous high-walled villas, fail miserably to connect. We do not map or connect them in any way. They are thrown into the air like bits of a jigsaw puzzle and left to fall as and where they will, in a state of utter confusion. Communities certainly do not connect. Neither do art, culture and the sciences, because there is no such thing with which to connect. In fact, nothing of importance to humanity ever connects, including life and death, the former of which is so cheap here. There is no bonding or connecting going on. There is a massive failure of connections – a nervous breakdown of essential parts. The only things that connect are submission and obedience to those who are pulling the strings – to the puppet masters – so there is no hope, you see, none whatsoever.

'We do not connect to one another as human beings, or to neighbouring Arabian countries who, as it happens, are also desperately struggling with their own failed connections, and having their strings pulled likewise. We may, once in a while, pay some lethargic lip service to change, but nothing very much ever changes for the better or at all, just as nothing actually happens to enrich our empty lives spiritually, emotionally or intellectually – apart from those materialistic petro-dollars that buy us the hollow consumerism that we mistake for civilisation. So our essential humanity is in a dreadful state of disconnection and dislocation, which is why this desert kingdom of ours is no place for life-loving human beings, least of all for those of the female variety. I pity us all and, for me, the kingdom is nothing more than one gigantic mental asylum of doom and gloom.'

Jalal is somewhat lost for words, but he manages to say, 'What a bleak vision you have, for such a beautiful woman.'

'That's because my beauty, femininity and womanhood are not allowed to connect,' she retorts, 'not allowed to connect beyond the veil where even my face is forbidden. Take it from me, Jalal, there are many women who feel as I do. I talk to them all the time. You men are denied the opportunity. You don't know what you're missing.'

Jalal tells Farida that, with the wealth that can be generated from oil, the desert kingdom can be transformed into a lush and civilised country, to be compared with the world's greatest centres of culture, but she does not believe him.

'It will never happen,' she says, 'because those who pull the strings here do not want it to happen. All they want is to line their own pockets. We already have enough wealth to embark on a transformation of the desert, but what do we do? We leave things as they are. We let sleeping dogs lie – mad dogs, most of them.'

'But,' says Jalal, 'some people regard the desert as a beautiful place to be preserved for future generations.'

'What is there to preserve?' she asks. 'What do we have in the desert other than too much sand and sun under an obtrusive and cruel sky? In the absence of rain, there is sun and nothing but the sun, a great downpour of sun that saturates and drenches all before it in an endless sun storm, flooding the great basin of sand that we call the desert, and soaking it to its roots, rotting its roots and drowning all growth and life in a mighty torrent and ooze of sun, blinding us with a great sheet of sun. I hate the desert. It is empty of life, of familiar sounds, of gardens, of people, of hope and of time itself. It is going to and coming from nowhere. It is one boring, monotonous and repetitive image with which to dull the mind and the senses, with which to reduce civilisation to a grain of sand and strip people of their emotions and their essential humanity. People who romanticise the desert and say that they like it there, cannot like themselves or life very much. Perhaps they hate life. Look at the Bedouin. They are not the noble savages that so many of the white Arabists pretend. They are ignoble, most of them, cutting each other's throats and doing whatever it takes to survive. Look at their sun-baked skins, deeply ingrained and coated with sand. They and their souls are soaked in sand. I don't believe that they like the desert. They have no choice but to make the best of a bad job.'

'What a townie you are,' replies Jalal, 'I must remember not to send you on any desert assignments. The desert is a part of our lives and we Arabians must reconcile ourselves to it.'

In due course, Farida writes her happy little column of domestic bliss, from her luxury home, visiting Jalal's office once or twice a week to discuss it with him, and to get to know the editorial staff, who are mostly British, and partly Indian and Arabian. She is the only woman in the office, and the men are, of course, attracted to her, like flies round a jam pot. Whenever she enters a room, so unaccustomed are they to a female presence, they cannot take their eyes off her. Some stand close to her, like cats hoping for a stroke, or trying to brush up against her, whilst others use any excuse to engage her in conversation. Asian and Western men alike are positively drawn to her. She is like a magnet to them and couldn't be more popular and, for all their inevitably lustful feelings, they respect her highly, for her mind as well as her body, for her gracious and civilising presence.

She has her own desk, so that whenever she is in the office she can do some work there if she doesn't feel like going home straight away, and the door of her office remains carefully and pointedly open at all times. Once in a while, a religious policeman looks in, when he is passing the office, to make sure that she is behaving herself, and Farida does her best to be civil to him for as long as it takes to get him off the premises, when she puts her tongue out at him behind his back, as he is leaving. Slowly, slowly ... Farida is becoming a liberated woman in the land of her birth.

But not for long, alas. Her column is published twice weekly and, by the end of the fourth week – the eighth column – Farida is in tears. The hate mail that she has received is unbelievably horrid, personally insulting and threatening. She is a loose woman, a Jezebel, a whore, a disgrace to her sex, her parents and the holy desert kingdom. She is an evil and unwholesome influence, and a bad example to other women, an unwelcome role model. No self-respecting woman should be writing a newspaper column, let alone working with men. OK, so she works from home most of the time, but no matter. She still goes among men to deliver and discuss her copy and, what is more, she is shamelessly attracting the attention of male readers by identifying herself with her column. She will want her photograph in the paper next! She hasn't even the modesty and decency to write her column anonymously, by using a pseudonym. She should be punished, she must be punished and she will be punished. She cannot be allowed to get away with such unseemly behaviour.

Well, that's what they say, her critics and detractors. Who does she think she is? What can she be thinking of, writing about such things as hobbies and pastimes for women, domestic and culinary matters, educational matters, children and baby matters, father and daughter matters, traditional Arabian clothes, travel destinations and so on? What a presumptuous woman! Why does she think that anybody could possibly care about what she thinks? Where was she brought up? Aren't her parents ashamed of her? Isn't she, when it boils down to it, just a common slut, a wayward daughter, attempting to disguise herself as a journalist? Perhaps she is some kind of troublemaker trying to upset the apple cart in the desert kingdom by championing women's rights. Well, she had better think again, because it won't do. She had better stay at home, if she knows what's good for her.

And stay at home Farida does. She is *so* upset – not least because some of the letters are from women – that she can write no more. She has suffered a massive loss of nerve and, as a result, her heart is no longer in it. She no longer has the stomach for it. She has run out of heartfelt passions. She feels utterly deflated, dispirited, hopeless and pointless. Despair has set in and she feels that it's not worth the effort, that she is wasting her time and getting nowhere fast. She has the restless and sinking feeling that she doesn't need this, and that she is being utterly *wasted*, all over again.

Before, she felt frustrated because of the sexual oppression, the lack of a job and the needless waste of her education. Now she feels frustrated because she has a job in which her talents and education are despised, in a country in which she has become hated to boot. She is weighed down with exhausting feelings of worthlessness, with mental and emotional exhaustion. She feels heavily empty, and that she is a waste of space, a waste of time, a waste of talent, a waste of womanhood, a piece of waste of no real value to most people, a waste product that is not wanted.

Jalal tells her, 'Listen, you are an excellent writer, so tough it out. You shouldn't pack it in now, just as you are beginning to get the hang of it. Given time, you can become a proper journalist. That's what you want, isn't it? So don't give in so easily. For every one who sends you hate mail, there are several others out there who are enjoying your column. Think of them. Don't let the bastards who send hate male get to you. Don't lose heart.'

'I have already lost heart,' she replies. 'A woman needs to be appreciated, you know, as, I imagine, do most journalists. But if there really are people out there enjoying my column, as you suggest, why don't they bloody well write in and say so? Maybe there are even more people out there who hate me, but cannot be bothered to write in and say so. Maybe I am hated more than I realise. Fifty hate letters a week, in the first month, is too much. I am staggered. I can take a hint, Jalal. I'm off. Damn them. Damn them all. Some of the letters are not only personally abusive, but very threatening, not only to me, but to my poor dear family. It's no longer worth the risk. I was hoping that this country had moved on since I came out of Cairo University, but it has not done so. I've had it. I'm finished. No more columns from me.'

She is right, because shortly after Jalal has advised her to ignore the hate male and tough it out, he gets a phone call from his friend, the Minister of Information, saying, 'Sorry, Jalal, Farida's column will have to go. I've had the royal palace on the phone with a message from the King, instructing us to drop it. Some quite important high-ranking people have made complaints to him personally. So there's no knowing where it will end. She's a marked woman, Jalal, and so, too, are her family for not putting their foot down and preventing her from disgracing herself, as her detractors see it. So it's time to pack it in. Of course, we never expected such an adverse response, but the idea has well and truly backfired, I'm afraid. Please give my sympathies to Farida.'

And so Jalal abandons Farida's column. But he tells himself that it was worth a try and that it might have come off, and he manages to persuade Farida to write one last column before she finally severs her links with his newspaper, this time on the taboo subject of women and their veils. In the belief that they might just as well be hung for a sheep as a lamb, he says to Farida, 'If that's their rotten attitude to women who dare to publish perfectly harmless and inoffensive articles in our newspapers, let's give these complainers something real to complain about for a change. Instead of bending over backwards not to write anything that can possibly offend them, let's hit them where it hurts, since they are going to hurt us, come what may. Give them a piece of your mind on the subject of the veil, Farida, since you cannot be in more trouble than you are already, and they cannot think worse of you than they do already. Go down fighting and have your revenge on them before you go.'

The subject of the veil is very close to Farida's heart and she has resisted writing about it previously for fear of upsetting too many people and losing her column in consequence. But what the hell! She is losing her column anyway, having done nothing to deserve it, so why not take her revenge in such a good cause against those who write her poison-pen letters? Why not tell them what they most need to hear and what she would have much preferred to tell them in the first place? Where has all this pussyfooting got her? Why should she respect the feelings of her vile detractors when they obviously have no respect for her feelings? Yes, she will do it. Jalal is right. She should go down fighting, and what a parting shot it will be, hitting her enemies where it hurts. What an offence to all women they are.

Already she is feeling better about her desperate plight. At least she will have written one column that was really worth writing, before she is through.

In her last column, Farida says that Arabian women wear the veil more as an empty symbol than a seriously held traditional belief, more as a sop to their men than a preference of their own. And she reckons that this is obvious from the fact that, whenever educated Arabian women travel abroad, they hardly ever choose to wear the veil, clearly demonstrating their indifference to facing strange men, which is not a problem for them. On the contrary, she observes that it is a problem for Arabian men, not their women, and she adds that a growing number of women are already dropping the veil and showing their faces to counter staff and salesmen when shopping in supermarkets and elsewhere in the desert kingdom. In due course, she predicts that the veil – and the *abbayah*, long, black maxi-dress – will become a thing of the past, a worn-out symbol of national dress rather than a traditional belief much beloved by women, that men's wishful thinking would like it to be. If women were allowed to vote, Farida argues that they would not vote for those men who insist that women should wear the veil and the *abbayah* at all times. She also asks Arabian men to consider the long, frustrating battle that women are up against daily in the desert kingdom where, instead of being regarded as a power trying to help their men, most women are treated as if they were enemy prisoners and slaves.

Reminding Arabian men of what a waste it is to ignore their women, she says that young women should have the same chance that young men have of having a good library and teacher, and she points out that the desert kingdom's recent admission of women to its universities is not such a liberating thing when it still insists that its brightest and best must continue to wear the veil. It's time, she concludes, for the poor lambs who regard themselves as men to grow up.

Well! One can imagine the alarm and furore that Farida's last column causes, not only to those who were already writing her poison-pen letters, but also to many others besides who had no serious objection to her column previously, but who are now beginning to have second thoughts, particularly if they are men.

But what does Farida care any more? She is on her way, having been deprived of her column already, without her telling any unpalatable and worthwhile truths in it. What more can her detractors do to this headstrong and shockingly beautiful young woman? Put her under house arrest and try to indoctrinate her? Let them do their worst. She is past caring and is feeling much, much better, having written something worthwhile at last, something explosive of which to be proud at last, while leaving her feminist mark on the annals of the desert kingdom's sexist history.

As it happens, Farida is not put under house arrest, and a year later she is married to a handsome young Arabian who shares her disgust with the desert kingdom, and has fallen in love with her from a distance, from reading her column. He is promising to transfer his wealth to London and live with her there before long. She has put her newspaper column behind her and cannot wait to escape to London with her husband. He is very handsome, university educated and such good company. She is happy at last. But from time to time, she and her husband meet people who remember that she wrote her ill-fated newspaper column, and so take it upon themselves to insult her. This is very distressing to her, not to say annoying to her husband, who is getting into too many arguments on his wife's account. Farida will never be forgiven in some people's eyes.

As for the American housewife – married to an American pilot working for the national airline – who has taken over Farida's column and is writing some predictably awful drivel for the interest of expatriate housewives, well, that's OK. She's not an Arabian, so she is no threat. She is not constrained by Arabian ideas of female decency. Nor can she be perceived as a challenging and inspirational role model to Arabian women, who may fancy their chances as journalists as a result of seeing what an Arabian female journalist can do. The American journalist can write as often and as much as she likes. No sweat. No worries. Nobody could care less. But let an Arabian woman try, and all hell is let loose.

A year later, Jalal is under house arrest again, having had his newspaper closed down by the authorities for a couple of days. He has been publishing articles allegedly embarrassing to the royal family and Government – articles about bribery and corruption in trade deals, the incompetence of high-ranking officials who ought to get their act together, the needless imprisonment of foreign lorry drivers involved in road accidents in the desert kingdom when they bring much-needed imports into it, Western doctors who exploit and rip off their wealthy private clients in the desert kingdom. That sort of thing. He is given a stern warning – 'next time we will have to close you down for good, so take more care in future what you publish. The Minister of Information may be your friend, but it doesn't mean to say that you can ignore all this good advice about what not to publish. OK?'

Jalal is also having staff problems. The British and Indian journalists are not getting on, with the latter complaining that the British are taking out all their pent-up prejudices and frustrations with Arabians on the Indians instead, for the simple reason that Indians are a much easier and safer target.

British journos are also given to drinking illegal alcohol after hours, and this is not helping matters. It can only be a matter of time before someone reports them to the religious police and has them arrested. The British are also seriously unhappy about the smell of Indian cooking in the block of flats that they share with their Indian counterparts, and they are always complaining to Jalal about power cuts — because some damn fool Arabian worker has put his pick-axe through a cable yet again — when they are under the shower, smothered in soap, but suddenly denied water to wash it from their hairy bodies! As for the stop and search that the Arabian police regularly subject them to, hoping for an excuse to drag them off to jail for not carrying their passports with them at all times, as they are required to do, the British and Indian journalists are equally fed up with this as well.

Like Farida before him, Jalal is beginning to lose heart, and he wonders if it's worth carrying on. He is having his ear bent every which way and he gets no thanks for having produced a Western-style English-language daily that is arguably the best in the kingdom. No thanks at all. He is a patient man, but there is a limit even to his patience. What the desert kingdom wants are sleepy and docile papers that obediently write uncritically and admiringly about the royal family on every other page, about government policies, sport, Arabian religious and other customs, and how wicked or seriously mistaken and incompetent Western and other foreign powers are. And they don't find much of this in Jalal's newspaper, getting only the bare minimum, in return for the government grant that is supposed to keep all papers loyal to the establishment.

Following Farida's example, Jalal packs it in, but, unlike her, he goes on a long holiday (Vermont and Switzerland are his favourite destinations). When he returns, he is horrified to discover that Farida's young husband has been stabbed to death. One of those who used to send her hate mail insulted her when she was walking along the seafront with her husband, taking the sea air in the cool of evening. When her husband thumped the man in question, the man's hot-headed brother stepped forward with a knife and plunged it into her husband's heart. Farida's young husband died in a pool of blood at her feet, while his murderer was marched off to jail, to be executed shortly afterwards.

As for poor Farida – the lovely Farida – she finally gets the message that it stands to reason, in the unlovely desert kingdom, that a woman had better know her place and accept that she is wasted. She had better resign herself to vegetating, and perhaps having children, just like 'normal' desert kingdom women everywhere. Otherwise, she and her nearest and dearest will be in serious trouble.

It is with a sense of needless but inevitable guilt that this message finally sinks in, wasting Farida further and further and further, and reminding her that her culture teaches one thing above all else, and that is obedience and submission.

11

TWO WOMEN LIVING DANGEROUSLY

Mrs Larson is kissing her husband on the cheek as he goes off to his office in downtown Jeddah. They live in the outer suburbs of this windswept seaport city where Mrs Larson stays home most days, dress-making, flower-arranging and preparing dinner for her husband in the evenings.

They are Swedes, but speak to each other in English most of the time and, as Mr Larson drives his company car away from their company-owned house, she waves to him from the kitchen window, before washing up the breakfast things and making herself another cup of coffee.

Her husband is summer-suited and booted in his air-conditioned car and office.

*   *   *

Mrs Shabokshi is taking a shower. Her husband has had his

breakfast and is on his way to his air-conditioned office in his air-conditioned and chauffeur-driven car. He is *thobe*'d and robed, but he has forgotten his worry beads, which he never fails to keep by him in his office, to help him get through the day. Likes so many Arabians, he likes to keep these beads in the palm of his hand and play with them while sitting behind his desk. The soothing effects of the beads are supposed to calm him, but now he is becoming agitated because he has forgotten to take them with him.

Mrs Shabokshi is famous for her all-female soirées at which Arabian women gossip and party, dance and flirt with each other, in the absence of their uninvited husbands, fathers and brothers, who respect the women's right to get together for some harmless fun on a girl's night out once in a while, driving their women to and from each of the soirées, but taking good care not to gate-crash them.

Mrs Shabokshi once had an American woman at one of these soirées who was persuaded by her and the rest of the Arabian women present to remove her skirt and knickers so that they could admire her pubic hairs. Arabian women are obliged to shave off their pubic and other body hairs, so they are naturally curious to see what these hairs look like on Western women.

For an Arabian woman, Mrs Shabokshi is unusual, not on account of her soirées, but on account of what she sometimes does and persuades other women to do at them. There are a number of women like her in the desert kingdom and they make their insecure men nervous, to say the least.

*   *   *

Mrs Larson is famous for nothing in particular. She has

finished washing up and is reading the daily newspaper and listening to the radio at the same time. She looks up at the clock on her kitchen wall before getting her head into her newspaper again. There is the usual daily photograph of the King of the desert kingdom, on the front page, with some caption beneath it reminding people not only of his presence, but of what a very good king he is. Mrs Larson turns the pages of her newspaper quickly, out of exasperation for something really newsy or interesting to read. After a while, she puts the paper down and goes upstairs to take a shower, leaving the radio on in the kitchen. She discards her dressing gown to reveal a short-legged woman, with a peachy bottom and a slender waist, with broad shoulders beneath short, curly blonde hair. She has a straight back and narrow hips and thighs and, turning round to look for the soap, she reveals small but ample breasts, a flat tummy and green-grey eyes.

* * *

Mrs Shabokshi is a big woman with pear-shaped, drooping breasts and a sagging bottom, long legs and wide, child-bearing hips with plenty of thigh. Her wet and shiny black hair is also short – unusual for an Arabian woman – but her tummy is not exactly flat, although her back is straight. She has flashing dark eyes and olive-coloured skin, and as this tall woman strides out of the shower in search of a towel, her breasts swing and her hips sway. She is like a boat in full sail.

Suddenly, her telephone rings in her bedroom, so she grabs the towel as she goes to answer it, walking naked behind her shuttered bedroom windows in the direction of the phone at the side of her bed, drying herself as the goes. But she is still dripping wet when she reaches the phone.

* * *

Mrs Larson is soaping herself under her shower and thinking of shampooing her hair. She is soaping herself between her legs and under her armpits, before moving on to her breasts, which she caresses gently after she has soaped them. Luxuriating under the water, as it tumbles gently on to her upturned face and streams down her body, she puts the soap to one side and reaches out for a bottle of shampoo, as she first wets her hair, before applying the shampoo and working it up into a rich lather.

* * *

Mrs Shabokshi is still naked and wet as she talks on the phone, listening to the voice of her husband who is ringing from his office to inform her that he has left his worry beads behind. He is asking if she will hand them to his chauffeur who is returning with his car in order to collect them. She says that she will do so and she reminds her husband that it is the chauffeur's day off, so her husband will need to book a taxi when he returns in the evening. 'Yes, yes,' says her husband, 'but he can come and get my worry beads first, and bring them here. It won't take him 30 minutes to repeat the journey.'

'It will take him 45 minutes,' Mrs Shabokshi points out, 'because it is 15 minutes each way and he must make the journey three times – here and back to you, and back here again to return the car before going home – but no matter.'

'Yes, yes,' says her husband, 'but he will only be losing 30 minutes of his day off, because he is being paid for the 15-minute return journey. Anyway, it cannot be helped, a man must have his worry beads with him in the workplace.'

Mrs Shabokshi agrees and puts the phone down, before drying herself thoroughly with her towel and then taking a hairdryer to her hair.

* * *

Mrs Larson has finished shampooing her hair and steps out of the shower to dry herself down, before going naked into her bedroom to apply the hairdryer to her curly locks. But she is interrupted when her telephone also rings and, when she picks it up at the bedside, it is Mr Larson telling her how much he loves her.

'I am naked,' she replies, to which he says, lowering his voice, 'In that case why don't you just lie down on the bed for a while and let me talk dirty to you?'

'Better not,' she says, 'these lines might be bugged for all we know and, anyhow, we are too busy for that, there's work to be done.'

'I can find the time,' he continues, 'but what is making you so busy today?'

Mrs Larson takes a deep sigh. She is, of course, very tempted. 'Listen,' she says softly and sympathetically, 'it's too risky over the phone in this country and I am busy making a new dress, remember?'

Mr Larson laughs and tells his wife not to worry. He will attend to her later.

She reassures him that she 'cannot wait', before taking the hairdryer to her hair again and then powdering her body.

Mrs Shabokshi has finished drying her hair and is powdering her body also, as she hurries to get back into her dressing gown before her husband's chauffeur reappears. She quickly locates the worry beads that her husband has forgotten to take with him and, when the chauffeur enters the drive, she is waiting at the door to hand them to him.

'I know it's your day off,' she apologies in Arabic. 'I'm sorry about this.'

'Not to worry,' he says, 'the traffic is not too bad, as it happens, so maybe it won't take too long. I'll leave the car in the drive and the keys in the ignition, when I return, and be on my way.'

She tells him, 'Fine, I'll retrieve them and hang them in their usual place in the hall for you to collect when you come for my husband tomorrow morning.'

He thanks her and proceeds to drive back to her husband's office once again, while Mrs Shabokshi returns to her bedroom where she steps naked once more out of her dressing gown, in order to dress for the day. For some reason, she decides not to put on any make-up today. This is unusual, because she likes to make her face up, before hiding it behind her veil.

* * *

Mrs Larson is already dressing for the day, having finally dried her hair and powdered her body, and she is climbing into men's clothes.

Standing in front of a mirror, she is straightening her tie and tucking her shirt into her baggy trousers, before zipping up her flies and fastening her trousers at the waist with a belt. Sitting on the side of her bed, she is bending down to pull men's ankle-length socks over her feet, before putting her little feet into nicely fitting flat shoes. Returning to the mirror, she lifts her short hair up at the back and the sides, and then clips it firmly over the top of her head. She also produces from her wardrobe a man's floppy cap, with a large peak, and puts it on her head, pulling it down to her ears on both sides, as she takes good care to push all her hair into the accommodating cap, peering into the mirror again to make sure that none of her hair can be seen at the sides or the back. She then puts on a light and loose-fitting artist's smock, turning the collar up at the back to meet the bottom of her cap, in case any of her hair should fall down, which seems unlikely in view of the fact that she has put plenty of hair pins and grips into it.

Needless to say, she is not wearing any make-up today.

* * *

Mr Shabokshi's chauffeur has delivered the worry beads to Mr Shabokshi in his office and returned his employer's car to his house, leaving it as arranged in the drive. He is walking off down the road, looking forward to his day off, which he intends to spend in bed with his wife who is waiting impatiently for him, stretched out on clean sheets, in their gently air-conditioned house. The chauffeur is in a hurry, as any man would be with a naked woman waiting for him. He lives at least a mile away from the Shabokshis, who seldom, if ever, stray into his neighbourhood, because it is a poorer area where they have no reason to go, and he has no reason to see them, therefore. Walking for one mile in the extreme heat of the desert kingdom is no joke, so he had better slow down if he doesn't want to exhaust himself, arriving all hot and bothered and sweaty. He does slow down, while his wife writhes restlessly on the bed, wondering what has happened to him and why he is running late.

* * *

Mrs Larson is also becoming restless, as she turns this way and that in her house, in these surprising men's clothes of hers, keeping clear of the windows in case anyone should look inside. She looks up at the kitchen clock again, before retreating into the hall where she straightens her tie in a mirror once more, before sitting down on a chair. She makes a very handsome man, with finely cut and sensitive features, and at first sight one would not think that she was a woman. The loose smock that she is wearing over her shirt is loose enough to conceal her shapely figure, so she looks the part, she really does. Apart from her woman's hands, she looks sufficiently male not to raise any eyebrows, and who spends too much time closely inspecting people's hands? It's not as if women are the only ones to have delicate hands and dainty fingers. Some men in soft jobs have them as well.

Suddenly, Mrs Larson hears a car entering her drive, so she springs up from her chair and peeps through the window at the side of her front door. A tall Arabian in a long and sweeping *thobe* is walking up to her front door, complete with headpiece covering the top and back of his head for maximum protection from the fierce sun.

Mrs Larson's heart is beating fast.

When the doorbell rings, Mrs Larson opens it apprehensively, and as she does so the Arabian steps into the hall, and embraces her passionately. The two of them go into a clinch and smile mischievously at one another.

Mrs Larson stands back and says to her visitor, 'You look magnificent.'

Mrs Shabokshi, who has also disguised herself as a man, in order to drive her husband's car round to Mrs Larson's house, replies, 'So do you, Mrs Larson. What a handsome little man you make. I could quite fancy you myself and take you off to my bed straight away. But we have things to do, I think.'

Mrs Larson giggles. She is not, of course, surprised to see Mrs Shabokshi in her house, disguised as a man. They do this once a fortnight, these two, and nobody has found them out yet. Because women are not allowed to drive cars in the desert kingdom, where the privilege is reserved for men only, so Mrs Larson and Mrs Shabokshi take matters into their own hands, by dressing up as men and taking to the open road once a fortnight in Mrs Shabokshi's husband's car. It is so exciting and thrilling and they look forward to it so much.

Both women are competent and careful drivers – more competent and careful than many of the men who regularly crash their vehicles in and around Jeddah – and they have a merry old time, driving round the streets and visiting some of their female friends who think them very brave and foolhardy. They also do a spot of shopping, disguised as men, in quiet backwaters where they are not likely to bump into too many people. Mrs Larson learned to drive in Sweden, before coming to the desert kingdom, and Mrs Shabokshi has been driving in Britain and the United Sates for years, both on holiday and while studying in those countries.

But they are flirting with danger. They know that. Should some fool of a man crash into them, they would no doubt be found out, as they would if a traffic policeman decided to stop them for whatever reason. And they – and perhaps their husbands, too – would be punished, if they were ever found out.

If Mrs Shabokshi's husband found out, he would probably exercise his right to beat her, whilst Mrs Larson's husband would very likely send her back to Sweden, for her own safety and in order to keep his well-paid job.

But in a country that is so belittling of women, some women are driven to desperate means to verify and assert themselves. Some women will take risks to overcome the stifling boredom and mighty insult to their daily lives. They will live dangerously to defy men.

Mrs Larson and Mrs Shabokshi are two such women.

12

WHITE ARABS

'It is not possible for a writer, who is not an Arabian, to get under the skin and into the mind and soul of an Arab, making him meaningful to the outside world. It is not possible for him to create a convincing Arab character in his fiction and provide a sense of what it is to be an Arab, how it feels and what it means. Only an Arab writer can do that.'

My Saudi Arabian colleague is lecturing me and I do not necessarily disagree with him.

'Of course, you can accurately write in human terms about beheadings and the stoning to death of adulterous women in an Arab country, because that is a subject that travels well, crossing borders and reaching out to all humanity – to hearts and minds everywhere. We can all imagine how terrible it must feel for any human being anywhere on earth to be beheaded or stoned to death, and no doubt there are some who can imagine it more powerfully and describe it in more detail than others. But Europeans cannot possibly imagine what lies behind that, what it is about the Arab mind, temperament, heart, attitude and feeling for justice and revenge that underscores that.'

'In other words,' I reply, 'the Arab mind is a no-go area?'

'It cannot be convincingly recreated and presented in an authentic way in European culture and literature because there are too many racial and cultural barriers and stereotypes to overcome, too many differences of blood and temperament and feeling, too many psychological differences. Arabs, likewise, cannot properly imagine what it must be like to be and to feel like a European. It's simply not possible.'

'You seem to be saying that Kipling was right, then – "ne'er the twain shall meet"?'

' "Meet" is the operative word. We can respect and tolerate each other's differences, of course, but in truth we can seldom meet or match them, because they do not fit. There can be no actual meeting of true minds between Arabs and Europeans, or any other races for that matter.'

'But we can, if we are of a mind to do so, transcend our differences. We can go beyond the limits of ordinary experience and travel into alien cultures and minds, and in that way we may come to understand and to feel what it means to be an Arab, European or any other foreigner for that matter.'

My colleague chuckles at this. 'But it would take a lifetime to do such a thing and few European writers have the time to spare. The trouble is, when we do sometimes manage to transcend our differences, we do not become more alike, as a result, we remain different for all that. We transcend by exploring the nature of the difference and doing our best to merge with it, but we can never leave our own very different culture and attitudes of mind behind, we can never shed our skin or abandon our hearts. So we do remain different. Arab hearts beat differently. They also hurt and wound differently where the emotions are concerned.'

'So, if we do manage to transcend, we are none the wiser in your view, but considerably better informed perhaps?'

'Exactly!'

'So what's to be done?'

'Nothing. We just have to accept that we shall never truly understand each other. Only by inter-breeding and mixing up the blood can such differences be properly transcended. But how many British and European writers who have written so extensively about the Arabs are of mixed blood?'

'None that I know of. Certainly not TE Lawrence, Gertrude-Bell, Philby or Thesiger.'

'Ugh! That pathetic bunch.'

'How do you mean?'

'I mean that in all their diaries and travel books these scholarly writers – "White Arabs" as the Shah of Iran so aptly called them – did nothing more than romanticise the Arabs out of all reality, recreating them in their own European image. They completely got the wrong end of the stick and, as for David Lean's excellent film, it is, of course, all about Lawrence of Arabia from a Western point of view, completely missing the point about the Arabs, as did TE Lawrence himself.'

'And what *is* that point?'

'That we are not in the least like Europeans and never shall be – that Europeans, for all their exposure to us, have no real sense of what it is like to be an Arab.'

'In his book, *Arabian Sands*, published in 1959, Thesiger

refers to the "greatness of the Arabs" and of the Bedouin who have "no thought of a world other than their own". He wrote his book as a "tribute to a once magnificent people" who were supposed to be vanishing under the "spoiling finger" of progress and time.'

This really gets my Arabian colleague going. He launches into a long tirade about Thesiger and Britain's White Arabs, much of which I cannot disagree with. But his argument is spirited and good natured and his mobile face creases into smiles and grins as he makes his various points, sometimes raising his eyebrows for emphasis, or looking astonished by Thesiger's claims. 'Thesiger was a child and a dreamer, an escapist from his own culture and the Western world, like so many of your White Arabs. More than a few of these "magnificent" vanishing people of his were bloodthirsty psychopaths and disgusting little bum-boys! Perhaps that was part of the attraction? A good many of the rapes on foreign women by Bedouin taxi-drivers in Jeddah these days are by these magnificent people.

'Have you seen how the Bedouin taxi-drivers, who have traded in their camels for a cab, swerve all over the road trying to kill cats and dogs as they pass them by? Have you seen how, in traffic congestion, they impatiently hoot and bump cars in front of them to hurry them along, before taking to the pavements and scattering pedestrians before them? Have you seen how they ask their Asian customers from abroad if they are Muslims, when they get into their cabs, and then slap their faces if they say that they are not? And what does Thesiger mean that the Bedouin have had no thought of a world other than their own? What is so virtuous about that? If we could only say the same for the grasping British! But we all know what kind of narrow-minded and unimaginative people never have a thought of any world other than their own. However, given the chance to think of another world these days, they happily pour into Jeddah, Riyadh and other cities, in search of a better life and higher standard of living – the sort of life that Thesiger could always return to when he got bored playing games out here in the desert, when he tired of regarding the Arabs as his playthings.

'I am so glad you mentioned Thesiger and these others, because they prove my point that there is no hope for the representation of Arabs in European culture. There is, believe me, much more to us than Thesiger and the rest of his privileged bunch were able to comprehend. I doubt that he understood his own lower orders, back in Britain, any more than he understood the Bedouin out here. Yet he is hailed as a great writer.'

We are sitting in a sexually segregated ice-cream parlour – with Arabian women at one end and men at the other – ne'er the twain shall meet! – and my colleague is really enjoying our conversation now that it has stepped up a gear. We have finished our ice-cream (which is remarkably good in Saudi Arabia), so I order some mango juice, while my colleague takes a breather, and I tell him that I do not disagree with him. He seems pleased to hear this.

'Is *Arabian Sands* still highly regarded in your country?' he enquires as he sips his mango juice.

'In certain quarters, certainly, and not least among Arabists and in diplomatic quarters.'

'That's predictable. Some people never learn. For all their understanding of our language, it seems to me that few Arabists really understand or care very much about us.'

'Yes, I get that impression, too. It's the language they are in love with.'

'But it's not only the British White Arabs who have got Arabia wrong in their time. Today's Americans are scarcely any better. They have an inclination to get up Arab noses by behaving in a crass way that suggests either that Arabs ought to be more like Americans, or that our "Arabness" is of little or no consequence to them. At least the British understood that we were different, even if they did romanticise it too much, but they were at least aware of it, and knew how to respect it. The American attitude seems to be that we Arabs are not as different as we think we are and, even if we are, we ought not to be.'

'You'll be singing Thesiger's praises in a moment!'

'I haven't read *Arabian Sands* for such a long time, but I remember it well.'

'It is an unforgettable book.'

He smiles to himself at this. 'But not for its shortcomings.'

'It has been described as a "really great book" and "the book to end all books about Arabia" according to Lord Kinross in the *Daily Telegraph*.'

'Really? I expect that's because of the British fascination with the Empty Quarter. I do hope you will write a book when you return to London, to remind people that Arabia did not "end" merely because these literary people said so.'

'As I told you before, I will do my best. I may surprise you one of these days.'

'Please do. I cannot wait. But don't try to create convincing or meaningful Arab characters, because there is no way, my good friend, that you will be able to do that. You need an Arab writer to achieve such a thing.'

'But your culture is not exactly friendly to writers.'

'Saudi Arabian culture is not friendly to them, that's for sure, but there are Arab writers in Egypt and elsewhere. However, I don't think that too many of them are translated into English, or widely read when they are. It's always the English writers who grab the popular imagination in England.'

After chatting about my plans to commit my own experiences to paper, I leave my Saudi Arabian colleague, as he orders another mango juice and looks longingly in the direction of the forbidden women at the segregated end of the ice-cream parlour, who exchange discreet looks and naughty glances with him, and tease him unmercifully as they drop their veils to eat their ices, licking their lips and their ice-cream suggestively for his benefit, as they smile at him from a distance.

Sexual apartheid is everywhere in Saudi Arabia, in restaurants, cafés and cinemas, on beaches and even in people's houses, where women are locked away from the men and their visitors on one side of the house, out of sight, but never out of mind.

I would like to tell more about my colleague, attired as he is in his long white *thobe* and chequered red headpiece, with the rubber fan belt that holds it in place. But I dare not, for fear of revealing too much about him, and giving him away to his enemies.

He has a point about Thesiger and the White Arabs. And the Americans, too. There is much to be learned still about the differences between Arabs and Westerners. To this day, there are still plenty of people who think about the Arabs in the romantic and unrealistic terms of the White Arabs. And there are few novelists and other creative writers who can create convincing Arab characters in works of fiction in European literature. Too often, the Arabs are reflections of ourselves or of the people we send into the desert to observe them – reflections that tell us more about ourselves, and our own culture, than they tell us about Arabs.

13

PALM TREE
AMBASSADORS

Once upon a time there were some ambassadors whose countries seemed to think that they were somewhat past it. They were thought to be over the hill and not exactly the best men for plumb postings in the great powerhouses of the world, in such glamorous and demanding places as Washington, London, Moscow, Peking, Tokyo, Paris, Bonn and so on. So when the Foreign Secretaries, to whom these ambassadors reported, ran out of ideas as to what, precisely, they could do with their unwanted diplomats, they called for their world atlases and globes, to see if they had overlooked some locations to which the past-it brigade could be sent.

First, they looked to the northern and southern hemispheres, in case they had forgotten any God-forsaken places there, to which these men might be sent and forgotten until retirement, but they drew a blank. So they began to cast their eyes in the direction of Latin America, Africa and South-East Asia instead. But there were no vacancies in these places either. Then somebody had the bright idea of narrowing the field down to the Arabian Gulf states, wondering how they could have forgotten such an economically important region in the first place – no doubt figuring that, apart from keeping an eye on the sleepy politics of oil, there wasn't much else for diplomats to do in that part of the world, where time moved so slowly that it sometimes ground to a halt and didn't move at all.

Yes! Without exception, these Foreign Secretaries all agreed that the Gulf States were the perfect dumping ground for ambassadors who had no prospects elsewhere. They, of course, came to this decision separately and at different times in their respective countries, and it was not until they got on the phone to one another about this and that, that the subject came up about the over-the-hill ambassadors, which is when they discovered that they were all on the same wavelength. They had all come to the same decision about where to get shot of ambassadors who were not in the top league ... or were even dropping out of the lower leagues altogether.

It wasn't that these ambassadors were useless exactly, but that they just weren't fast-track or cutting-edge enough to be the first people to spring to mind when a lively and demanding posting was on offer. They had their good points, nobody could deny that, but the good points that they had really were not good enough, so they had better be sent to the Arabian Gulf instead, and they had better not complain either.

Some of the ambassadors in question knew perfectly well that, far from being slightly past it, they were well and truly past it, so they knew better than to complain. They were quite relieved to discover that they were being sent to a diplomatic backwater somewhere in the Arabian Gulf, where they could nod off under a palm tree and snooze their way into retirement. It suited them down to the ground, it really did. So they were grateful for such a considerate posting.

But others were, truth to tell, definitely miffed, considering themselves to be much better than they were, and not liking the stigma that went with a posting in the Arabian Gulf, where they would be known, they knew perfectly well, as the 'palm tree ambassadors', not only among their own kind, but among disrespectful Arabs as well. They did not look forward to this and they felt aggrieved on account of it, and if they had always been too big for their ill-fitting little boots before the cat was let out of the bag about their not exactly being first, second or even third rate, they became even bigger for their boots now that salt had been rubbed into the wound by relegating them to the Gulf. They were resolved to show anybody who thought otherwise that they were by no means past it, so they became very defensive and they quickly grew to be even more full of themselves, more arrogant and more overbearing than they had ever been before. They became big (and somewhat ineffective) fish in a small pond, splashing around needlessly to see if they couldn't make some kind of impression and get rid of the stigma.

So there were two sorts of palm tree ambassador – those who were perfectly relaxed about the posting, who put their feet up and took it easy; and others who were very touchy and puffed out their little chests and inflated egos to see if they couldn't rise above the stigma.

Not that any one of the inflated ambassadorial egos in the latter category were foolhardy enough to try it on with the sensitive Saudi Arabians with whom they had good diplomatic and trade relations to preserve. Oh no, it was with their own communities, wives, families, members of staff and the media that they displayed their self-importance and aggression, given that they thought they could get away with it. They were overly snobby, these aggressives, and were usually to be found standing aloof, like prima donnas, presumably in order to show that they were people of some considerable importance, even though they had been consigned to the bottom of the ambassadorial heap. And they consistently overrated themselves, these sadly underrated men, as they made fools of themselves trying to demonstrate that they were not people to be messed around with, and that they were in no mood to suffer other fools gladly, or to be amenable to people of lower rank. They did not want to be bothered, if they could help it, with humble businessmen or intrusive journalists, or citizens from their countries of origin who may have fallen foul of the Saudi authorities and finished up in jail, rightly or wrongly. And they were very choosy about who their wives and members of staff put on their embassy guest lists. People had to ingratiate themselves into their favour and make sure not to offend their sensitive feelings in order to get on to and stay on their lists. There was a pecking order to be observed and there were appearances to be kept up.

For the sake of appearances they would be civil to a journalist from *The Times* in London – and they were vain enough to want to be quoted in that newspaper, which was read by most of their foreign office crowd and families, so they perceived the paper to be influential – but as for other journalists, including the local press, they were lowly curs and would be treated accordingly.

But the easy-going ambassadors in the former category, who had no hang-ups about being of the palm tree variety, and could handle the so-called stigma very well, were of a completely different sort. They were informal and much more relaxed and approachable and seemed to be enjoying themselves so much more than the others. Because they were not smarting like the others, they were having a ball, some of them.

The old Austrian Ambassador, for example, spent most of his time playing the piano for his wife, a retired opera singer, who sang for him in the kitchen, bedroom, bathroom and out on the embassy lawn, where she kicked off her shoes and danced around as if she was at a ball in Vienna. There were several grand pianos in the Austrian Embassy, where a number of diplomats also played the piano, and where parties were regularly organised for Austrians and others in the local community.

Both he and his wife had a great sense of humour and seemed to be making the best of a bad job during their posting in the desert kingdom. If they felt underrated or shunted out of the limelight at all, they showed no signs of it.

Nor, for that matter, did the middle-aged German Ambassador, who spent a good deal of time throwing dinner parties and savouring fine wine, while also listening to classical music when he was not reading about and discussing art and art history, a favourite subject of his. His favourite English-language authors were Virginia Woolf and Faulkner and he also liked Cervantes, this man who seemed to leave the discussion of trade deals and commercial relations to his commercial staff, who were doing rather better than most of the foreign contingent at competing for Saudi business. The German Ambassador, meanwhile, got on with passing the painfully slow time in the desert kingdom reading good books and cultivating hobbies and friendships with interesting people. One could not fail to like his style.

The Swedish Ambassador was different again. He was in his middle years and spent much of his time scribbling away, writing murder mysteries and detective books that were published back in Sweden under a pseudonym, and his head was full of all manner of fictional ideas and plots for bumping people off and throwing policemen off the murder trail. Being a writer of fiction in his spare time, he took a keen interest in people of all sorts, doing his best to read their character, and he, too, was very approachable.

Both the Pakistani and Indian Ambassadors were well advanced in years and, like the senior members of their staff, they were perfectly charming, and they held splendid *durbars*, with all sorts of tasty Indian foods on offer, and attractive sari-clad women in attendance. Both ambassadors liked nothing better than to invite people to dinner for a good gossip and a laugh about the Saudi Arabians and the local diplomatic community in Jeddah, which they took with a large pinch of salt. They were interested in all things English, of which they had a good knowledge.

But the Indians were somewhat put out by the fact that the Saudis were deporting Sikhs from the desert kingdom because they found their turbans insulting to the Muslim religion. Because the Sikhs are forbidden by their religion to remove their turbans, they were marched on to boats by Saudi policemen in the port of Jeddah and sent back to India. The Indian Ambassador suspected that the Pakistani Ambassador had put the Saudis up to this, pointing out to them the religious symbolism of the Sikhs' turbans and reminding them how offensive this was, a charge denied by the Pakistani Ambassador, of course.

Taking the view that the Pakistani Ambassador wanted the Sikhs out of the way, in order to make room for Pakistani workers instead, the Indian Ambassador argued that it was

Saudi Arabia's loss because the Sikhs were much better and more intelligent workers than the Pakistanis.

The young Canadian Ambassador (of Polish origin) was an absolute joy. He could not have been sent to the desert kingdom because he was past it, because he was too young, so perhaps he was there to cut his teeth and gain some experience. Very approachable and always prepared to spill the beans off the record about anything under the sun, he had a great sense of humour and loved gossip.

As for the smiling South Korean and cheerful Taiwanese, they, too, were perfectly happy to be palm tree ambassadors in their middle years.

The Taiwanese Ambassador was a model of perfect behaviour at all times, he was a relaxed and kindly old soul, who loved to play golf for hours on end on local golf courses with imported grass, and drink plenty of whisky within the safe confines of his Embassy and home. Like the South Korean, he was very generous with his whisky, disguising bottles in brown paper wrappings, so that special guests and friends from outside the Embassy could take one away with them without being seen by the police.

While the stuck-up ambassadors, who did not identify with this easy-going group, spent most of their time being stuck up, some of them did have their moments, and one – who behaved very much like an elder statesman – was chief among them. He could occasionally be caught in a good mood and, on such occasions, he managed to come over as a convincing human being, this man who, according to the palm tree theory, was not otherwise all that convincing as an ambassador. Because he was an accomplished Arabist who could not only speak Arabic, but read it as well, he was remarkably well informed about the history

and culture of the Arabs, most of whom regarded him as a spy –
as they do any non-Muslims who have taken the trouble to speak
their language.

In his book, *The Diplomats*, Geoffrey Moorhouse observes
that 'it is a truism of the diplomatic life in any country that a
nation sends its most talented representatives to those places
abroad which, for one reason or another, are of the most
concern to it', and that the policy in Arab countries of 'treating
the locals ostentatiously as equals and trying to get the most
out of it' will 'sound to some much more like the fawning of
Uriah Heep'.

It is not difficult to understand that, when a Lion Heart finds
that history is against him and that he is perhaps expected to
behave like Uriah Heep, he may not be in such a good mood
with himself or his country much of the time.

On the other hand, if the easy-going palm tree ambassadors
can adjust to it, why not the others as well? Because, very likely,
the easy-going types are not Lion Hearts.

But one should drink a toast to them all. They have a job to
do, just like the rest of us.

14

A DAY AT THE
CAMEL RACES

Her Majesty Queen Elizabeth II greets the Arabian King on her royal yacht, which is berthed for the occasion in one of the desert kingdom's deep-water ports. She does not set foot on Arabian soil, but welcomes the King on to her yacht instead, and he is very pleased to accept her Government's invitation to meet her and her unpredictable husband, the Duke, who has a reputation for diplomatic gaffes on royal tours and state visits when – in his spirited but somewhat misguided attempts to be friendly – he has occasionally made inadvertently racist jokes and clumsy remarks that have gone down like a lead balloon.

At the suggestion of the British Ambassador in the desert kingdom, the Foreign Secretary respectfully advises Her Majesty the Queen not to enter the kingdom, on account of its undignified handling of women. The Foreign Office has it on good authority from its ambassador that the Arabian King is not capable of treating Western women with the respect that they deserve, including perhaps on a royal visit, so it would be better, in the circumstances, for the Queen to stay on her yacht where the situation can be controlled from her point of view. It seems that the Arabian King is quite capable of treating women with contempt, regardless of the consequences. This has already been reported in the Sunday Times, *much to our embarrassment and the embarrassment of the Arabian King, so it may be advisable for Her Majesty's press secretary to contact the editor of the* Sunday Times *to see if we cannot put a stop to further leaks of this kind, presumably by one of our Embassy staff in the desert kingdom. Perhaps the suggestion should be made for the young Prince Charles to visit the* Sunday Times, *with a view to showing him how a newspaper is put to bed, thereby presenting the Prince with an opportunity to have a word in the editor's ear, to see if we cannot establish the source of this report, and persuade the* Sunday Times *not to publish any more embarrassing reports of this nature, at least for the time being. David Owen, the Foreign Secretary, is very put out.*

The Arabian King is tall and and somewhat overweight. He is being presented to the Queen of England who is short and plump, and she is shaking his hand and welcoming him aboard. She is talking to him about something or other while he appears, bless him, to be doing his best to pay attention to what she has to say. He wouldn't normally bother to listen to a mere woman, but needs must, and at least he is not doing so on his own sovereign territory. He is on the Queen of England's royal yacht, after all, so he should at least have the courtesy to pay attention to his host, if only for the sake of appearances. Perhaps he thinks to himself that she is an upstart woman who ought to be left at home, while her perfectly charming husband, the Duke, represents her in a man's world.

It cannot be denied that it is a bit off for a king of the desert kingdom to have to kowtow to a woman in public, and it will take him a little while to live this down. Maybe he is wondering why it is that wimpy British men are so humbled by their women, deferring to them as they do, and even allowing them to become queens and prime ministers once in a while. It could never happen in his country.

Her Majesty the Queen would like to know from her Foreign Secretary what is meant, exactly, by the Arabian King's 'undignified handling of women'? In what way is he undignified and not capable of treating Western women with the respect that they deserve on state or any other occasions? Her Majesty would like to remind her Foreign Secretary that she is no ordinary woman and more than capable therefore of knowing how to deal with an Arabian king. Could she please have more details without delay and, in particular, would the Foreign Secretary kindly provide a full explanation of what it is that Her Majesty's Ambassador in the desert kingdom, Sir John Wilton, has reported to the Foreign Office. As for the suggestion that Prince Charles should visit the Sunday Times, *Her Majesty believes that this is a perfectly splendid idea, and the press secretary has the matter in hand.*

The Arabian King and his entourage are being led into the royal dining room where a sumptuous banquet awaits them. It is a grand and glittering dining room such as you might expect from the wealthiest and most glamorous royal family in the world – wealthier than all the European royal families put together. The King understands that, bearing in mind the foods that he and his entourage are not allowed to eat for religious and health reasons, the menu has been carefully selected, with the help of advisers from his own court, so he is feeling relaxed about having to dine at a non-Arabian table. He is glad to be seated between the Queen and her husband, so that he won't have to spend the entire evening talking and listening to a puffed-up woman. It will be good to have the conversation of her husband as well, racist jokes and clumsy remarks notwithstanding, and the King is looking forward to discussing horse-racing and hunting with the Duke, two subjects in which both men have a common interest. But he does hope that the Duke won't suddenly say anything really daft and embarrassing, such as 'do you still stone adulterous women to death in your country?' or 'Have you chopped off any interesting heads recently?'

The Foreign Secretary regrets to inform Her Majesty that her well-respected Ambassador in the desert kingdom has reported that its king has treated the Ambassador's wife, Lady Wilton, in a very undignified manner. The Ambassador has written a long letter to the Foreign Office explaining how this came about, and a copy of this very detailed letter will be hand-delivered to Buckingham Palace today for Her Majesty's consideration. Her Majesty's husband, the Duke, knows about this matter, because he was witness to the indignity in question, but perhaps he has forgotten to mention it to Her Majesty. But the Foreign Office cannot forget it, because the indignity that Lady Wilton has suffered seems to be as insulting to Her Majesty's royal household and the British Foreign Office as it was to Lady Wilton, the Ambassador's wife, and this does not augur well for Her Majesty's royal visit, which is why Her Majesty's Foreign Office agrees with Ambassador Wilton that it is most advisable that the Queen of England stays on her royal yacht while she is in the desert kingdom.

The food at the banquet is perfectly splendid and the Arabian King and his entourage have enormous appetites. Seated on the other side of Her Majesty the Queen, one place removed from the Arabian King, is the British Ambassador in the desert kingdom, Sir John Wilton, who seems to be enjoying himself. The Arabian King pays him many compliments, for the benefit of his superiors, the Queen and the Duke, telling Her Majesty what a pleasure it is to do business with Sir John, and how perfectly he speaks Arabic, unlike most ambassadors in the desert kingdom. The Arabian King says that British Arabists are widely admired by his people for their ability to speak Arabic so well, and for their detailed knowledge of the kingdom and its ancient culture, which they seem to understand so much better than most. The King congratulates the Queen on having the best diplomats in the world and adds that both countries are well served by such admirable men. Britain's long history in his part of the world is not to be underestimated, in the King's view.

To the Duke, the Arabian King has much to say about horse-racing and hunting, and with regard to the latter he has a very interesting conversation with the Duke about hawks, which are popular hunting birds with Arabians. He tells the Duke that, in his royal palace, he has magnificent paintings of hawks and stallions, by his court painter who, as it happens, is British, and does all the royal portraits, as well as paintings of animal life. He studied at one of the best art colleges in London – the King cannot remember which one – and he has since become very rich, painting for the desert kingdom's royal court. Whilst his critics say that his shiny oil paintings are perfectly ghastly, and far too chocolate box for their liking, as far as the Arabian King is concerned, his British painter is absolutely the cat's whiskers. He has painted some seriously impressive portraits of the King himself, in various poses and situations, all of which do justice to his royal personage. What a pity it is that the Duke and the Queen do not have time to visit the Arabian King's royal palace, for he would love them to see these paintings and, indeed, to meet the court painter. Had this banquet been arranged at his royal palace, instead of on Her Majesty's yacht, the Arabian King would have been pleased to show these paintings to the royal couple before the evening was through. But, as it is, his royal palace is more than one hour away in a fast aeroplane.

Clearly, the evening is proving to be a great success, and the English Queen and the Duke appear to be having a rattling good time. As for the Arabian King, he doesn't seem to mind too much to be conversing with a foreign Queen, although it is true that he is more at ease with her husband, probably because, man to man, the two can find more to talk about. The thing is about these royal visits, they are not difficult to pull off and, being carefully stage-managed, the participants know perfectly well what is and is not expected of them. They realise that they have a part to play for an appreciative and programmed audience that will not fail to applaud, providing everyone keeps to the script and remembers their lines. Both sides are there to entertain and charm each other, and to reassure one another that all is well between them and will continue to be so in future. A state visit is party time with canned laughter, and therapy time, too, and its celebratory purpose is to massage egos and to detract from (and perhaps reward) the hard bargaining and squabbling that may be going on behind locked doors at lower levels, where the diplomats must apply their skills backstage, and can, if necessary, be left to carry the can.

Her Majesty the Queen wishes to inform her Foreign Secretary that it won't be necessary to copy Sir John Wilton's letter to her at Buckingham Palace because she has now had an opportunity to find out from her husband the Duke what it was that he neglected to tell her on his return from his recent visit to the desert kingdom, when he met with Sir John and the Arabian King, in order to plan her royal visit in advance and to put the necessary arrangements in hand. The incident in question was indeed regrettable and completely lacking in dignity and decorum, so Her Majesty is in complete agreement with her Foreign Secretary that, when the royal visit eventually takes place, she will certainly stay on her royal yacht.

The Duke did not forget to mention this incident to the Queen. On the contrary, he took the view that it was best not to mention the matter, for fear of putting the Queen off making a visit that urgently needed to be made, for obvious reasons, or making her nervous in any way. So he remembered not to tell her. He took the diplomatic view that it was better to say nothing and let sleeping dogs lie on this occasion, since none of us wants a diplomatic incident with the desert kingdom. Whilst Her Majesty agrees that the Arabian King's disrespectful and harsh treatment of Lady Wilton, in the presence of her husband

and no less a person than the Duke, is unforgivable – and she wishes to send her sympathies to Lady Wilton for it – she also agrees with the Duke that it is not worth making waves and risking a diplomatic incident. Nor is it worth the loss of face that would inevitably result if it became known that the Duke had been unable to do the gentlemanly thing and prevent the Arabian King from insulting the British Ambassador's wife in the presence of a distinguished member of the British Royal Family. There would be a serious loss of face if the Duke had to admit that all he could do was take a deep breath and swallow his very considerable pride, no doubt choking on it in the process. Better, therefore, to keep Mum about the humiliation of the British Ambassador, his wife and the husband of the Queen of England.

Of course, the Duke did not expect a subsequent letter of complaint to the British Foreign Secretary from Her Majesty's Ambassador, Sir John Wilton, and it may be that Sir John is disappointed in the Duke for not having made a stand on behalf of Lady Wilton. But that would have risked a diplomatic incident.

However, now that Her Majesty's Ambassador in the desert kingdom has resurrected this matter, the Duke agrees with the Foreign Office that it would be better for Her Majesty the Queen to stay on her yacht when her royal visit goes ahead. The Duke would also like to send his good wishes to Sir John and Lady Wilton, and to thank Sir John for his efforts on behalf of Her Majesty's Government in such a difficult country as the desert kingdom. The Duke would also like Sir John to know that he enjoyed his company and looks forward to seeing him again in the near future.

After the royal banquet, the British Ambassador and the Duke are having a large brandy together, following the departure of the Arabian King and his entourage. The evening has been a great success and new trade deals that are in the pipeline will be quickly signed on the orders of the Arabian King who has much enjoyed being sucked up to in such a regal manner. Her Majesty the Queen has retired to her room and the Duke has asked the British Ambassador to join him for a nightcap before he makes his way back to the Embassy. Both men are haughty beyond belief and, being broad-shouldered and very tall, they have a startling and inescapable way of looking rather as gargoyles do, peering down from the top of high walls and buildings. Predictably rather full of themselves, with the kind of pride and straight-backed deportment that befits their respective stations in life, they walk tall these two, and they also drink plenty of brandy besides.

'So, all's well that ends well,' says the Duke. 'What a business it all is. How much better it was in the days of Empire, when all we had to do was send in a gun boat.'

'Quite so, your Royal Highness,' says Sir John, 'but it's a different ball game these days, now that history's boot is on the other foot. Understandably, the Arabians quite like making us grovel for a change, but I do think that the King went too far with my wife when you were last here.'

According to the Duke, the Arabian King 'ought to have been horse whipped for such unmanly conduct'.

'How is your wife, Sir John?' the Duke asks. 'Did it make her ill, having to sit out in the sun on that uncomfortable bench, with only a newspaper over her head for protection?'

Sir John explains that his wife was indeed sick after her ordeal in the sun. 'It made her giddy and, when she returned home, she went straight to the bathroom to be sick. It's no joke being exposed to the sun for a couple of hours in such excessive heat. I couldn't believe my eyes and ears when the King instructed his minders in Arabic to bundle my wife out of his royal box. I could see that your Royal Highness didn't realise what was going on until it was too late, since the King was speaking in Arabic, but I must say that I expected better behaviour from an Arabian King and his entourage in the presence of a British royal.

'Of course, I understand that Arabian men are always required to leave their wives behind when they have diplomatic or business receptions to attend with others – that is their custom, I realise that – but I did not expect the King to apply such a ridiculous rule to my wife on the occasion of your visit. I rather expected more respect for *our* customs for a change. My wife was dying to meet you and she was looking forward to being with us in the King's royal box. Instead of which, she finished up outside, sitting on a bench and holding a newspaper over her head because she was exposed to the scorching sun! It was nothing less than a bloody disgrace.'

'Of course it was,' the Duke sympathises, 'and it was a damn silly idea to go to the camel races in the first place. I'm not interested in seeing camels racing. It's horses that interest me, not ugly, smelly camels.'

Sir John agrees. 'Yes. But one needs to be able to master a camel and ride it in the desert, in order to get the respect of the natives. I occasionally ride a camel at weekends, but I agree that it's not anywhere near as comfortable or exciting as riding a horse. It was the King's idea, of course, a day out at the camel races. Camel racing is very popular here and the desert kingdom imports camels from nearby Cairo and distant Australia. It's quite a sight when camels are unloaded from boats in the docks, where cranes connected to hoists have the lanky beasts swinging in mid-air, as they bring them down on the quayside. The King wanted to show you something very different, by taking you to the camel races, and he wanted to teach me a lesson for daring to suppose that I could bring my wife with me, into his royal box for once, just because a member of British royalty was visiting. I ought to have known better. But I was persuaded by my wife that an Arabian king could hardly object to her presence when such a high-born royal was visiting from Britain. But we got it wrong, I'm afraid, and he objected like hell. You should have heard his filthy language in Arabic. It was perfectly foul and deeply insulting. Arabian men are very touchy about women and you never know which way they are going to turn. I don't know if you noticed, but the King's men wouldn't even allow my wife to travel in any of the cars that were reserved for us. She was supposed to be travelling in your royal car, with you and me when you arrived at the airport, but they wouldn't let her anywhere near it.'

The Duke pours himself and the Ambassador another large brandy. 'No, I did not notice anything, I'm afraid. So how did Lady Wilton get to the racetrack without a car? Don't tell me she took a camel!'

The Ambassador replies that his wife 'had to grab a taxi and follow the royal procession, chaperoned by one of my embassy staff'. and that 'she had to return home afterwards by the same means'. He reminds the Duke that it is not beyond the realms of possibility that even the Queen of England could, in her innocence, inadvertently cause offence in the desert kingdom, without realising it, which is why he wrote to the Foreign Office pointing out that it would be a lot safer for Her Majesty to stay on her royal yacht.

The Duke remarks that he sees that the Ambassador has taken care to leave his wife at home this time, even on the Queen's royal yacht, to which Sir John replies, 'Oh yes ... once bitten, twice shy. She couldn't bear the prospect of being in the presence of the odious Arabian King again.'

'What a business it all is,' says the Duke repeating himself, 'when a British ambassador cannot even take his wife along with him for a day out at the camel races with a member of the British Royal Family. How times have changed.'

'And not for the better,' says Sir John, 'not by any stretch of the imagination.'

'But how is your wife now?' the Duke enquires. 'Perhaps we can meet her at last? How about tomorrow morning, when she might care to join us for breakfast, before we pull out of here?'

'Afraid not,' says Sir John rather awkwardly, 'she has had to return to London for ... ahem ... some urgent hospital treatment.'

'Oh dear,' replies the Duke, 'nothing too serious I hope.'

The British Ambassador's usually confident and haughty face is suddenly full of unaccustomed blushes. 'She is in need of some blood tests, having been bitten by a rat that came up the loo and bit her on the bum. And she is also in need of a long-overdue break from this atrocious country.'

The Foreign Secretary wishes to compliment Her Majesty the Queen on a successful royal visit to the desert kingdom, the tangible results of which have already come to fruition in the form of yet more signed contracts for British companies, according to Her Majesty's Ambassador in the desert kingdom, who reports that the Arabian King has not only confirmed this on the phone to him, with his thanks for a splendid royal dinner, but has also sent his warmest wishes to Her Majesty and His Royal Highness.

Following the visit of the Queen of England to the desert kingdom, it is rumoured that the Arabian King, for all his apparent shortcomings with the weaker sex, presented Her Gracious Majesty with a golden palm tree statuette, complete with black coconuts, to the value of some £4 million.

So honour is satisfied all round.

15

ALL HAIL TO THE
HOUSE OF SAUD

When a tribal family goes into the Arabian desert, conquering all who stand in its way and calling itself royal, people take notice. From one end of the country to the other, they take notice, as do neighbouring countries and the world at large. Word gets around.

It is not often that a single family rises up, out of medieval obscurity, to build a nation in its own image, and to give that nation its own name, as it puts itself and its country on the world map, when history could so easily have passed it by. History cannot point to many examples of such families. So the mighty achievements of the House of Saud are not to be underestimated.

Theirs is one hell of a story – the stuff of Hollywood films, no less – and it is a story that is not yet finished, as the family continues to sink or swim in the twenty-first century.

The House of Saud is – or rather, has become – Saudi Arabia through its own turbulent history and amazing determination, vision and extraordinary willpower, financed and armed from the start by the British, whose protectorate and puppet kingdom it willingly became, until such time as it was ready to fly the nest.

While Britain conveniently looked the other way, this family massacred other tribes and grabbed their lands, until it created a desert kingdom for itself, inventing itself in its own image with its own bloody hand, mastering its own destiny and making its own fate in the name of its God and its religion.

Few would belittle such an accomplishment. What the House of Saud has achieved is, to say the least, mind-boggling. It has made its mark like no other and puts its breathtaking stamp on history, with a whole country named after it, carved out of the desert in its own style, with a corporate image and logo all its own. Imagine a United Kingdom named after the House of Windsor!

One can readily understand the mystique and allure of the House of Saud in the minds of its admirers – Europeans and Arabs alike, not forgetting the White Arabs, of course – but one can also understand that it is bound to have jealous enemies and many of them.

With tribal roots, allegedly going back to the eighteenth century, here is a family that has withstood the test of time, that has defied the tides of history that have not always been in its favour. Here is a family that has listened to the winds of time and heard and read them better than most. This fledgling royal family – only 75 years old – has not only turned itself into royalty, it has also turned its country into an oil-rich kingdom that can sometimes throw its weight about on the world stage, capturing the imagination of the world in the process. It has sent its sons to Western universities and military colleges and it has bought itself a string of palaces and mansions, strung like a necklace of pearls across the Western world.

Here is a country that has known how to suck up to the right rather than the wrong people in this world. Having sucked up to the imperial British instead of the Turks, in the days of Empire, when Britain was powerful, it then sucked up to the United States instead when it became the major world power. But it modelled itself on British royalty and it was British royalists and Arabists who originally taught it royal ways that were not only strange to it, but which it took the family time to get the hang of. It is said that the founding vagabond king, Ibn Saud, who lived in a tent, thought that the world was flat and that the Americans were Red Indians. And it was British royalty who invited members of his vagabond family to Buckingham Palace where it could take a deep breath and sniff the royal air for itself.

Having imported royalty from Britain, the family also set about importing an ancestry for itself, this time from Egypt, from where it took an Egyptian scholar to research and write a lineage for it (to cook the books, according to the family's critics), as it set about making itself respectable for a change.

Nobody denies that all this is an astonishing achievement, one of the most remarkable achievements known to history and the Arab world. So you have to hand it to the House of Saud, it has done remarkably well for itself, very well indeed, and many would argue that it has done even better for its tyrannised people.

The story of how it has done all this has not been told. Forget David Lean's excellent *Lawrence of Arabia* film. That was only the tip of the iceberg. There is so much more to this story from an Arabian and world point of view, as history melts down before our eyes and we see that there is so much more to the Arabs and Arabia than Lawrence of Arabia and the imperial British ever knew.

The question for any film-maker interested in the House of Saud would be whether to approach it from the angle of a mafia family or from the point of view of a royal family. Alternatively, it could be seen from both points of view, of a mafia family that turns itself into a royal family, giving a whole new meaning to respectability and how it is developed along the corridors of power, and providing an extra Arabian dimension to the Italian concept of mafia. No doubt about it, this story would make a great film.

Or course, interested film-makers would have to decide what to do about the political prisoners reportedly taken, tortured and murdered by the House of Saud, but that's no problem for Hollywood producers and directors who are well used to dealing with mafia tortures and murders, which make for great entertainment. And then there are those who say, 'So what if this royal family has tortured and murdered a few of its opponents along the way? Which royal family hasn't? In a violent part of the world, where justice is very rough indeed, what do you expect? Life goes on, royal and mafia families go on, so be glad that this extraordinary Arabian family envisaged and fantasised itself into a royal role, when it could have chosen other less noble paths.' This is what a good number of people say. There is always hope for royalty in this world, they believe.

So all hail to the House of Saud, then. It would be churlish in the extreme not to acknowledge its great accomplishment.

It has its place in history and it has, to some extent, dragged itself and its country out of the middle ages into the modern world. On the other hand, it can be accused of keeping too much of its country in the middle ages still, of resisting democracy and social reform, and preventing its 'backward' people from going forward into Arab nationalism and perhaps even socialism, all of which is anathema to the House of Saud, which knows only one kind of nationalism, and that is its own brand of Saudi nationalism.

But if its people really are so backward, why then does this royal family need to keep such a grip on them? Maybe they are not backward at all, this *nouveau riche* educated class of merchants, retailers, shopkeepers, consumers, engineers, academics, business and military men – these former Bedouin tribesmen – maybe they have their heads screwed on perfectly well and would just like a little more democracy and a little less dictatorship.

Should the House of Saud fall in the twenty-first century – as some have predicated that it will – then it will only have itself to blame for not having moved with the times, for having been too greedy and corrupt, for not having embraced democracy and social reform in a world in which most affluent and educated people, such as the Saudi middle classes, demand nothing less.

But if this family that has already invented itself once out of nothing and from nowhere can reinvent itself once more, then the chances are that there will be a Saudi Arabia for ever, and that Hollywood films will be made about it before long.

This family has made history once, so let it make it twice now, and make it better than before. The story of the House of Saud is the story of how to make a country, how a family takes fate into its own hands and makes history in its own image (with the help of some powerful friends).

16

SINISTER TOURISM

'*Roll up, roll up, this way for Jeddah Pier, you lucky people. Are you enjoying your holiday in Saudi Arabia? Of course you are!*

'*Now hurry along there, and don't miss the beheading that is about to take place here. It's the tourist experience of a lifetime, come along now, don't be squeamish, most people love it, you will, too.*

'*If you don't fancy a beheading, at the far end of the pier, stop off in the tunnel of love at this end, because we're stoning an adulterous woman to death in there, and you may prefer that to a beheading. Come along now, don't be bashful, all human life is here, it's here for the taking, believe me, you'll never get a chance to see such things again, seeing is believing, that's what they say, isn't it?*

'*What's that, darlin', you'd like to see both? No problem, my dear. I can give you a discounted price on a ticket for both, and I think you will find that it's excellent value for money. This must be your lucky day.*

'*Should you also like to take in the chopping off of a thief's hand, and fearsome lashing of a man's back, until his blood-soaked skin is raw to the touch, I can give you a very special price. I really can. Come over here, my dear, for the bumper offer of the week – a real bargain price.*'

Tourism of this sick and sinister kind is not beyond the realms of imagination. It is not inconceivable. OK, not in the above form perhaps, but in a desert kingdom that is slowly getting round to opening itself up to tourism, to lifting its traditional ban on tourists from the outside world, tourism raises the question of Saudi Arabia's darker side.

What, other than its sinister darker side, does it have of interest?

The answer is that the desert kingdom has very little, of course. The holy cities of Mecca and Medina are out of the question, yet the Saudis are, believe it or not, considering how best to package the desert kingdom as a tourist destination. The kingdom's famous coral reef springs immediately to mind – it is beautiful, apparently, and has already attracted visitors from the outside world – as perhaps do desert safaris. Then there are the royal palaces, the fabulous wealth of which a lot of tourists would no doubt like to see, but, other than that, there really isn't much to attract tourism.

But there is the sick attraction of Saudi Arabia's enormously sick attractions, and we do know that, after the Vietnam War, European and other tourists paid good money to visit the battlefields, so why wouldn't tourists pay to see a public beheading in Saudi Arabia, or the chopping off of a thief's hand for that matter, not to mention the stoning to death of an adulterous woman? Why wouldn't those who visit the London Dungeons, the Chamber of Horrors and places like that not visit places of real horror in the desert kingdom?

And why wouldn't the Saudis include this in a tourist package?

After all, once you have tourists roaming around your streets at will, they may very well happen upon and see these things anyway, unless you take good care to police their movements and keep them well away from such things.

And if tourists should happen upon these ghastly things, the Saudis would very likely want to bend their ears on the matter in order to justify their barbaric punishments, and this could be done a lot better in an organised tourist group, with a group leader to control the happy holiday-makers and make quite sure that all the best propaganda is put over to them while they are watching heads roll, hands being severed and stones raining down on defenceless women.

But this is going too far, some will say, not even the medieval Saudis could be so brazen and distasteful as this. Surely they would not stage-manage such inhumane and revolting acts for the benefit of tourists. Surely they would not cash in on the death and savage punishment of their convicts in this way. For heaven's sake, they must have other more palatable tourist attractions than this. Well, they stage-manage these events for their own citizens, so why not tourists also?

And as for the desert kingdom having more palatable attractions, well, now, let's see. They have pubs with no beer and hotels and restaurants with no wine, unless the Government opens up specially designated hotels and restaurants to booze in order to attract tourists. Then there are endless miles of sand, with some Bedouin camps that might perhaps be visited. And there are the coastlines, as well as sexually segregated ice cream parlours, beaches and cinemas. There are also the oil fields. What a great tourist attraction they would make!

Come now, hand on heart, what does the desert kingdom really have to offer for the interest of the outside world, other than its darker side?

Most of its traditional architecture has disappeared under bulldozers and concrete. Its food is nothing to write home about and there isn't any wine to help wash it down. The extremely hot weather is appalling to all but a few masochists. And in most, if not all, of the places that one visits, there is a ban on photography, because fundamentalists are supposed to regard cameras and photographs as the devil's work.

When I first went to the desert kingdom, I was not aware of this, so I tried to take a photograph of children playing football. When the children realised that I was taking photographs of them, they stopped playing football and started to pick up stones and throw them in my direction. As the stone-throwing increased, it became clear that, if I did not make myself scarce pretty fast, I, too, may go the way of an adulterous woman and be stoned to death. So I jumped into my car and drove away from the sandy football ground at speed, chased by stone-throwing Arabian children.

One can well imagine the horror of unsuspecting tourists, arriving in Saudi Arabia with their cameras at the ready, suddenly finding themselves being stoned!

Saudi traditionalists rule tourism out completely. They do not want 'heathens' – and especially heathen women – coming into their country from the outside world and lowering the fundamentalist tone of the country. They do not want them putting temptation in the path of Arabians and opening their eyes to what Saudis are missing. They do not want their filthy foreign influences. They do not want car hire for female tourists in a country in which women are not allowed to drive cars. So they think that tourists are more trouble than they are worth.

OK, maybe these traditionalists can be persuaded that carefully controlled tourist groups visiting designated areas and under strict supervision can be trusted to keep themselves to themselves, and not wander off the beaten track, contenting themselves with holidays in tents near Bedouin camps, or with underwater snorkelling holidays and a view of the coral reef. But they really do not want foreign tourists roaming in and out of *souks*, rubbing shoulders with ordinary people, and getting an eyeful of all the atrocious and embarrassing things that are going on in the desert kingdom today. They do not want them spreading the devil's propaganda of democracy, or giving Saudis the idea that there is nothing wrong with drinking alcohol, taking photographs and being happy. This is the kind of forbidden life that Saudi Arabia's rulers and upper classes reserve for themselves in the outside world, as far away as possible from the desert kingdom, out of sight, so they certainly do not want it turning up on their doorstep and letting the cat out of the bag for all to see.

No! Tourism, apart from a few furtive visits here and there, and on a limited scale, is a no-no in the desert kingdom, so forget it.

And forget all that twaddle about 'sinister tourism' with a view to turning the desert kingdom's barbaric and inhumane punishments into a tourist spectacle for sickos from the outside world.

'Allo, 'allo, 'allo, what 'ave we got 'ere. A group of foreign tourists,

SINISTER TOURISM

I do believe. Well this won' do. It won' do at all. Oo gave you lot permission to enter this country? Where are yer passports and yer tourist visas? Yer don' 'ave 'em on yer? Well yer should. Yer not allowed on these 'oly streets of ours, unless yer do. Yer should know that. Don't yer know nuffin in the outside world? Yer really should 'ave remembered to bring yer papers with yer, and it won' do, I'm afraid. It won' do at all. Yer required to carry 'em at all times, so I'm goin' to 'ave to arrest yer. Yer nicked. I'm goin' to 'ave to let yer see a bit ov life be'ind bars in this precious country of ours, in the land of the pure. Yer'll enjoy that, I'm sure.

17

THE SILLY GOOSE AND
ITS GOLDEN EGG

It is obvious – even to someone who knows little about the desert kingdom – the relationship that we must foster with Saudi Arabia and why we must continue to support it in this wicked and absurdly hypocritical world of double standards and tragic mistakes.

The kingdom of Saudi Arabia may very well be a tragic mistake, but there is nothing that we can do about that, so there's no point crying over spilled milk. It is important to the economic and social wellbeing of the world order (and not least to the West) that Saudi Arabia's bountiful oil supplies – which were discovered and made possible by the West – do not fall into the hands of others even more fanatical and unreasonable than the extreme and backward Saudis; others who very probably would be hostile to the West – as, indeed, Iran has proved to be since the Shah.

So we may conclude from this that the latter-day fact of Saudi Arabia, whatever we think about it, cannot be helped, which is why we had better make the most of it, and help ourselves into the bargain! We need oil supplies to be safeguarded and supplied at the right price, just as we need the lucrative trade deals and Saudi investments that, like the oil, flow towards us.

We should not apologise for being self-interested in this grossly self-interested world. The Saudis understand this very well, so we should not mince our words on this subject. And when hypocritical British journalists put politicians on the spot on our television screens and ask the inane question, 'How can you support Saudi Arabia?' – as if they didn't know, our politicians should be in a position to reply, 'Come off it, stop asking dishonest questions, you know perfectly well why we have to support Saudi Arabia, circumstances being what they are, which planet do you guys live on?'

There is also the possibility that the Saudis will eventually implement the social reforms that the West and others would like to see, in the not too distant future, if we continue to stand by and support the desert kingdom, taking care to bend its ear on these delicate matters. And it is important that we *do* bend its ear, on a regular basis, otherwise nothing will ever change for the better, and things could go badly wrong and change for the worse in their part of the world if we and they don't watch out.

But most important of all, there is the Western-educated – British- and American-educated – Saudi ruling class, some but not all of whom are not anywhere near as bad as the country and people who have spawned them. These are not unreasonable people – they have come in the mould of the former Oil Minister, Sheikh Yamani, and others – and we have no choice but to place our hopes on them and our trust in them. Some but not all of the Saudi ruling class are not only reasonable, but intelligent, courteous and decent with it. They are people who have their hands full at home, and who may be our best hope for the future. They deserve our support for as long as we need to support them, and for as long as they need our backing in this marriage of convenience in which we find ourselves, since the British, followed by the Americans, ventured into their part of the world, in search of oil and to keep the Turks out of Arabia.

We cannot, as yet, afford to throw away that part of our history – of Saudi history – however much we may wish to see a different Saudi Arabia than the one that confronts us today. And while there are those in the Saudi ruling class who are all too obviously self-serving, power-obsessed reactionaries and fascists, we should remember that all ruling classes have had such people, including our own.

Most British and Western diplomats and ambassadors would privately agree with this – as would a number of politicians – but they are not likely to admit to these things in public, so they will continue to be trapped into saying one thing, whilst secretly believing another.

Saudi Arabia is, in many ways, an unpalatable fact of life – a nasty taste in the mouth – but we had better get used to it. It is also a perfectly understandable product of its own history, as are we and other nations. But it still needs to reform, to stop dragging its feet, so that it can become more democratic, humane and pleasing to its people and the outside world. So we should not shrink from saying to the rulers of the desert kingdom, either privately or publicly, that they need to understand that any criticism from Britain and the West is intended to be constructive and emanates from a friendly part of the world that happens to care for the kingdom and its people – when it is not caring about its trade deals and oil! The West has come to know and to understand it, but cannot go along with so many of its mistaken and inhumane ways in the new millennium.

Saudi Arabia also needs to understand that the time for a grown-up relationship is long overdue, and that we can no longer just accept and actively support the status quo, as our diplomats and leaders have done previously without question, for fear of upsetting it. Rather, we can welcome it into a new and mature relationship for the future, in which we will, of course, support it for obvious reasons – just as it will accept our military and moral support for obvious reasons – but that we and its subjects will find life a great deal more comfortable if it changes some of its medieval ways.

While, in the opinion of Saudi Arabia, these medieval ways may be none of our business, we need to remind our Saudi friends that they are the concern of all in the civilised world who believe in a humane and civilised approach to these age-old problems, by which we have all been plagued in our time, and by which the Saudis will continue to be plagued if they do not change their mistaken practices, and break loose from their history.

And while we understand that Saudi pride is at stake, we should remind them that we have our pride, too, and that if we are to be proud of our Saudi ally, then perhaps the time has come for a little less Arabian pride, and a little more common sense from here on.

We have no choice but to support Saudi Arabia, which, likewise, has no choice, if it knows what is good for it, but to listen to us once in a while. But thus far, our grovelling diplomats and cautious politicians have been too scared to say 'boo' to the Saudi goose, which has become a silly goose in consequence of laying such a marvellously golden egg.

The belated message to the Saudis in the new millennium must surely be: don't be a silly goose all your life. You may be the goose that laid the golden egg, but this egg of yours does not give you the right to be silly for ever. No harm can come to you from listening to reason once in a while, from lightening up once in a while, instead of behaving like the pampered babes – the spoiled brats – of the Arabian world.

Silly goose? That's an absurdly false analogy, isn't it? It's a bit more serious than that, wouldn't you say?

Oh yes, it is much more serious than that, but as in Orwell's *Animal Farm*, these livestock analogies can be very effective. When, for example, a king claims his country's income for his own, and a Western power (the United States) is so dependent on him for his oil surpluses (to keep the price down and the flow uninterrupted) that it gives a nod and a wink to his fundamentalism, in order to keep nationalism and socialism out of the desert kingdom, there is something very silly indeed going on, especially when that fundamentalism rebounds on the United States both on Sept 11th and in Afghanistan where the USA fanned the flames of fundamentalism to keep out the Russians. This really is silly goose time, big time. And the biggest and silliest goose of all may yet be the King and his royal family, should they, too, not be able to contain the flames of fundamentalism that they have manipulated, and which may rebound on them, just as it has rebounded on the USA.

If we wish to have any influence with Saudi Arabia at all, we won't achieve that by being too scared to use our influence honestly and fearlessly, and frankly tell the Saudis what we think, in the nicest possible way, of course. It's tough love they need, not soppy excuse-making and refusing to grasp the nettle.

And if we wish to protect the goose that lays the golden egg, then we need to protect the goose from itself, as well as from its enemies.

Plain and friendly talking is what is required from here on between consenting adults.

18

FLEETNESS OF FOOT

An Arabian comes in the night with fleetness of foot and a cane in his hot little hand into a torture chamber.

He has come before, but is returning once more to indulge his sadistic pleasure by means of torturing a man who has been falsely accused and wrongly imprisoned.

The first time he came to a British prisoner – a white-collar worker – he said, 'Take off your shoes and socks and put your feet up at the end of the bed.' The poor man wondered what he had done wrong, having been snatched at random from the street as a suspect of ... what? It was anybody's guess.

The Arabian says this to all his prisoners, as they bow to the inevitable and accept their unenviable fate, deciding not to argue for fear of angering their false accuser. They have no choice. What else can they do?

At the foot of the bed, the cane-wielding torturer, who has

come so eagerly and with such fleetness of foot, proceeds to deprive his defenceless victims of *their* fleetness of foot.

They have not seen the last of him. He will return, this grinning psychopath, again and again. He enjoys his work, this spiteful, screwed-up little man, who is so miserably low on humanity and astonishingly high on brutality, and he looks forward to repeating his handiwork as often as circumstances permit. But what is *wrong* with him? What kind of culture and collective attitude of mind spawned him? Did civilisation pass him by? Has he no heart? This guy is into other people's pain like some people are addicted to drugs. But what is *wrong* with the mental health of the desert kingdom that empowers him?

Don't ask, just endure, and hope against hope for the best.

That part of the human body on which we stand or walk is both crucial and delicate. It is our means of mobility, and it is delicate because of its soft-skinned underside that is sensitive to the touch. It is no secret. Being sensitive, it is in need of protection if we are to stand or walk properly or at all. Outside temperate climates, intense heat or cold are unbearable to the soles of the feet.

There is something about the feet that appeals to the warped imagination of this Arabian who has come with a cane in the night. There is something about them that he cannot get out of his head as they fester away in his consciousness, intriguing him to know how far he can go with his victims, some of whom can take more than others, and all of whom are coerced into a desperately demeaning and paranoid relationship with him as he beats the soles of their feet and asks them questions, as he talks them through their agony and breaks them down. *'Will he? Won't he? Yes, he will. Oh my God! What can I say to* appease him? Am I guilty? I thought I was innocent. No, I must be wrong. Yes, I am guilty after all. I must have done something very wicked to have deserved this. Please forgive me. No more beatings please.'

Being sensitive, our soles are, like tender hearts, in need of gentle and careful handling. Stroked and massaged gently, our soles can have a soothing effect with which to relax us – when tickled they can have an unnerving effect – as they connect with and relieve the pressure points elsewhere in the body. By the same token, they can have an acutely painful and crippling effect when treated cruelly or harshly, when viciously beaten with a stinging cane or other implement. We can be crippled emotionally and psychologically as well as physically. There is a nervous breakdown awaiting us all in the abused and misused soles of our feet.

Because our soles are one of the most sensitive areas of the body that are the least resistant to pain, the desert kingdom authorises (or turns a blind eye to) the beating of the soles of people's feet inside its jails, either to punish or torture them, or to make them talk and so confess to things that they have not done. To our knowledge, there are currently four or five Britons behind bars in the desert kingdom confessing to crimes they appear not to have committed.

Recently, a Welsh accountant was falsely accused and wrongly imprisoned in the desert kingdom, where he suffered this barbaric torture in a jail, before being released and returned to the UK. We also know that there are countless others in desert kingdom jails where it is widely rumoured that they are having the soles of their feet beaten.

It is hard, if not impossible, for most people to imagine the kind of excruciating and deeply penetrating pain that one suffers from these merciless and heartless beatings. It is a repetitive screaming pain that whistles through the body like a sharp-pointed arrow with jagged edges, not once, but time and again, giving rise to a great mental suffering and emotional anguish and distress that accompanies the splintering, physical pain. It is a vicious, crippling pain that puts a victim's nerves on edge, as a sharp-toothed instrument of torture bites into the souls of his feet, taking great chunks out of his resistance and pushing him and his nerves over the edge.

This vile and devious torture insults and distorts the psyche as well as the body, in its degrading attempts to be utterly soul-destroying and soul-deforming, as it inflicts a severe mental as well as a physical pain on its victims, hurting and maiming them so much that they may say or do anything that is asked of them – confess to almost anything. At this point, the torturer's undignified and repulsive handiwork has not been in vain; he has put in another good day's work of which he can be proud, leaving his victim with an excruciating and insufferable pain that is by no means fleeting, either now or in the fullness of time.

Arabians will tell you that there are worse forms of torture than having the soles of your feet beaten, and this may very well be true. But let's not be glib, this is a truly ghastly and hideous form of torture that the desert kingdom cannot deny and should immediately ban if it wishes to keep company with the humane and civilised world that is rightly sickened and appalled by such grisly and shameful acts.

Let's not be squeamish. Let's ban it, along with the public beheadings and floggings, stonings and hand amputations. These punishments and tortures are a sensitive moral and

political issue, of course, but it's time to become civilised and
humane for a change.

19

A Faustian Pact

Once upon a time there was an Arabian tribal chieftain living in a desert land where he was lord of all he surveyed in a remote backwater. He was a regional chieftain at odds with other chieftains in other regions, each of whom were, like him, lord of all they surveyed, which was very little.

Then, one day, some British explorers, business and military men came along, offering modern weapons to this chieftain and his Bedouin warriors in return for their keeping the Turks out of his neck of the woods, where the British reckoned they had sniffed the desert air and smelled oil, the mind-boggling wealth of which would soon transform the chieftain's life into one of hitherto unimagined luxury.

The chieftain warmed to their vision of sumptuous wealth and luxury. He also wondered why the British couldn't fight the Turks for themselves, until they told him that they were engaged in a much wider war where they had bigger fish to fry, but that they would deal with the Turks in due course, and not for the first time, after he had resisted them on their behalf in the interim.

Not being entirely stupid – even though it is true that he thought the world was flat and that the North Americans in far away USA were Red Indians – this tribal chieftain soon realised that, armed to the teeth with British weapons, he might conquer all the other regional chieftains, once he had dealt with the Turks. He might even find himself ruling over a whole country instead of a mere part of it.

Of course, this would mean killing a fair number of his fellow countrymen and their respective leaders, but he reckoned that, since they were inclined to kill each other anyway, there was no reason why he should not finish them off once and for all, if that's what it took to become the supreme leader of his disunited country. Why not, when such a glittering prize as kingship beckoned?

Kingship was an unfamiliar word that had been whispered into his ear by the British who, as everybody knows, had long known all about kings and queens, so the chieftain figured that perhaps these pale faces were not as stupid as they looked if they could equip him with the arms with which he, too, could join the royal gravy train of the outside world and become a king rather than remaining a mere tribal chieftain. Yes! He quite fancied being supreme ruler of his desert land, instead of carrying on as a down-at-heel regional upstart from the back of beyond. So he made friends with the British and did their bidding, until, at last, he turned himself into a king, lord of all he surveyed for as far as the eye could see, not just in the obscure region from which he came, but throughout the country at large, which he was vain enough to name after himself and his family; while his British friends were crafty enough to make him into their puppet king, in return for his keeping safe and secure the future oil that they had sniffed in the desert air, and selling it to them and their Western allies at a favourable price that suited their pockets.

It was at this point that the former tribal chieftain-turned-king came to discover that the North Americans were not the Red Indians that he had supposed them to be, when they eventually came calling from the USA with an astonishing shopping list for oil supplies that would guarantee him great wealth for many years to come. It suddenly dawned on him that it was the Americans rather than the British who would make him wealthy beyond his wildest dreams, so he gradually transferred his affections to them, but taking care to let his British friends down ever so gently, of course, because without their help he would not have become supreme ruler. Cosying up to the Americans at every opportunity, he soon got a taste for their way of life, and he and his successors sent many of their people to be educated in their country.

Everything was turning out really well for this tribal leader-turned-king until he was reminded by a bunch of fanatical hot-heads who had helped him conquer his country that he *owed* them – that he had, in fact, made a Faustian pact with them.

These hot-heads were religious zealots and ruthless warriors, renowned and feared for their ferocious cruelty and barbarism, and known as Wahhabis. It was they who had helped him to slaughter his fellow countrymen in order to conquer and suppress them when he first came to power, and it was they who then became his personal bodyguard, protecting him once he was in power, so that he, his family and entourage could sleep safely in their beds at night. But they could turn against him at any time and overthrow him, if they took it into their heads to do so. But they would not do this as long as he honoured the pact that he had made with them, which was to give them the very *soul* of his newly built country to dominate as they sought fit.

Being fanatical religious zealots, regarding themselves as God's holy warriors on earth, these Wahhabis were great collectors and abusers of other people's souls.

While the soul of his country was certainly not the king's to give, he nevertheless did not hesitate to offer it to the Wahhabis, in order to save his own skin and enjoy the colossal privileges of kingship and, in doing so, he said farewell to his own soul as well.

But his people did not, of course, thank him for this. Many of them already felt cheated, deeply resentful and badly insulted by his family's hijacking of their country by immoral and illegal force and Wahhabi terror tactics. Having initially resented that he had stolen their country from under their noses, many of his people felt doubly insulted now that he was presuming to add insult to injury by hijacking their souls as well, and handing them over to the *diktat* of the despised Wahhabis. This new ruling class not only told them how to live and how many times a day to pray, but punished and tortured them severely and sometimes fatally for all manner of so-called sins and alleged acts of immorality and/or political dissent.

While the king enjoyed the trappings of his new-found power and wealth, the Wahhabis relished their religious fanaticism and enforced it viciously. So honour, such as it was in these deplorable circumstances, was supposed to be satisfied all round.

The pact that this self-appointed king had made with the Wahhabis was truly Faustian because it enabled them to spread their fanaticism and terror wherever they went, imposing their obscenely puritanical and barbaric religious laws on the people, in return for their keeping their hands off the king and privileged members of his charmed circle (many of whom were self-appointed royal princes by now). Having agreed to fight alongside this former tribal chieftain in the first place and help put him on the throne, the Wahhabis felt perfectly justified in insisting upon nothing less than the precious soul of his country, drinking the people's blood at will. They objected to the drinking of alcohol on moral grounds, but they had no hesitation in drinking the blood of the people, and this was the price that the king had to pay in order to carry on being king.

And pay it he did, without conscience, so corrupted was he by his new-found power. It was also part of the deal that, while his people had to observe Wahhabi laws and religious practices – to which the king also, of course, had to pay lip service – he and his family were at liberty to ignore these practices in their private lives, and sin to their hearts' content, as long as they did so in secret and kept their double standards to themselves.

The Wahhabis had a long-standing and intolerant hatred of infidels and other religions, not least the Christian religion, against which they were always prepared to wage a holy war at the drop of a hat, and it angered them that their king was in hock to the Christian countries for his and their new-found wealth and power. But they were shrewd enough to see that their riches and influence could come from no other source. Even so, at the first opportunity, they would dearly love to be shot of the despised Christian world, and to crush it if they could, so they quietly contented themselves with spreading their festering hatred against it in neighbouring countries.

Their condemnation of the Christian faith spread far and wide, as far as such places as Pakistan and North Africa, where there were many other religious fanatics who greatly admired and feared these religious fundamentalists, seriously believing them to be God's holy warriors here on earth to fight the good fight against all sinners and infidels, including the United States of America. There was no reasoning with the intolerant and vicious Wahabbis, who saw everything in black and white, and they were, like self-righteous bigots everywhere, never prepared to turn the other cheek, or to take a philosophical, humane or forgiving view of those who happened not to agree with them.

While the Wahhabis were delighted to have the soul of their country fall into their laps, they were not overjoyed at having to put up with Christians in their country doing business with their king and bringing their modern influences with them, so they regularly reminded the king that he should watch his step if he knew what was good for him. And knowing what was good for him, the king let the Wahhabis have their way with his people, because he suspected that this was the best way of controlling and appeasing them, preventing them from rising up against him for having stolen their country from them – because he thought that this was the only way of maintaining his power base.

Suffering under the brutal treatment of the Wahhabis, and the systematic destruction of the soul of their land, many ordinary people revolted, attempting to win back the right to self-determination, justice and tolerance. But the Wahhabis were too powerful, and all resistance was easily crushed.

The thing about a Faustian pact is that men who seek great earthly powers at the expense of their immortal souls usually finish up damned, unless, of course, the devil with whom the pact is made has the tables turned on him (as in the case of Faust himself), so that he becomes the one who is condemned to eternal suffering. But, thus far in our story, the vicious Wahhabis with whom the king has made his pact remain triumphant and victorious.

Eventually, the king and his princes grew old and died of

natural and not so natural causes, only to be replaced by their heirs who continued to honour the pact that had been made with the Wahhabis and other fanatics, into the new millennium, enabling them to become more and more powerful, amusing themselves by telling the people how to live their lives, and terrorising and torturing them in the process.

Then, one day, a puritanical and God-fearing young Arabian man – who had been born to one of the many wives of one of the old King's best friends – grew to adulthood and became the desert kingdom's most notorious son. He also became the world's most wanted man. This is because, having swallowed the Wahhabis' religious beliefs and fervour hook line and sinker – and fancying himself as the holy ruler of the desert kingdom in place of its puppet kings – he used his enormous wealth to recruit fanatical Arab terrorists, encouraging them to become suicide bombers on his behalf in a holy war that he declared on the United Snakes of America for having overstayed its welcome in his country.

Since his father had been one of the old king's best friends – having become a multi-millionaire when he was graciously favoured with the lucrative building contracts for the refurbishment and expansion of the holy mosques in Mecca and Medina, and subsequently when he helped to build the desert kingdom's infrastructure – this devout and God-fearing man was seriously rich. But he was also seriously obsessed with Wahhabi fanaticism and religious hatred. So he thought nothing of recruiting, training and financing suicide bombers to hijack some aeroplanes and fly them into the World Trade Center in New York, killing more than 2,000 innocent civilians of all nationalities and religions. He lived up to his reputation as the desert kingdom's most notorious son, as well as the world's most wanted man, when American and British troops set out to track him down, while their air forces bombed his mountain lair in Afghanistan, where he had gone to help other fanatics wage a holy war against the Afghan Government that was not puritanical enough for his liking.

In Britain, the Bishop of London said that there was not a shred of justification for the suicide bombings in New York, and that justice demanded that the reality of their evil should be recognised.

Ironically, the world's most wanted man had originally gone to Afghanistan to wage war on the long-standing enemy of the 'United Snakes' – the Russians – who were invading that country for reasons of their own, and he had initially received the financial backing, military support and approval of both the Americans and the royal family of his country, who were keen to see him and his religious zealots succeed in keeping the Russians out of Afghanistan. They had no objection to his taking Wahhabi warriors with him to turn their hatred against the Russians. Probably, the royal family felt somewhat relieved that there were fewer Wahhabis on their backs at home, now that so many of them were off to Afghanistan. But when, after the eventual expulsion of the Russians, the desert kingdom's most influential zealot joined with others to set their sights on the post-war Government of Afghanistan, helping to replace it with a new religious dictatorship of their own, it was at that point that the Americans and royal family of the desert kingdom began to wonder what he might do next.

And what he did next – with his so-called Arab–Afghans – was help to rule Afghanistan with an iron fist, while also giving the nod to the unleashing of a barrage of insulting abuse on his own country's royal family, suggesting that it should ditch its American ally or be overthrown. And then, to cap it all, he declared a holy war on the Americans and their allies, bombing and killing the latter in Africa and anywhere else in the world where he could catch them on the hop. He did all this in the name of his Wahhabi religion, even though he was not in any way qualified or sanctioned by his scriptures to declare a holy war.

After the bombing of America's World Trade Center – which he claimed he had done to send a powerful message on the subject of Israel and the Palestinian cause – he made a celebratory video in which he and his Afghan colleagues were seen sipping Turkish coffee and joking about the success of the operation.

But he had gone too far, as such people are inclined to do, and when American and British troops turned up in Afghanistan to confront him and his Wahhabi and other warriors, he and they quickly retreated. He went underground, probably into hiding in Pakistan where he had many friends and admirers, or perhaps somewhere in Iraq. Nobody seemed to know. Some said that he had been killed by American bombs, but this was not generally believed by those who wanted his head. And while he was on the run, his Wahhabi followers returned to the desert kingdom from which they had come to resume their former role as the king's personal bodyguard and ruthless suppressors of the people; until such time, no doubt, as the Americans forgot about the world's most wanted man, so that he could quietly return to his home land through a back door that the Wahhabis would perhaps keep open for him. He might then be in a position to forge a new Faustian pact with them, overthrowing the royal family, and becoming the kingdom's first religious dictator, with the Wahhabis' blessing.

Some people tried to argue that the desert kingdom's royal family had already sold its soul to the Americans, so there could be no question of its having made a pact with the Wahhabis. But this was clearly not the case, because the deal that the royals had struck with the Americans had never been in exchange for their souls, let alone the sacred soul of their country. That particular deal had been done with the Wahhabis. On the contrary, the American and Western worlds had always shown much more consideration and respect for the desert kingdom's religious customs than ever the kingdom had shown for theirs.

Meanwhile, in Afghanistan, the so-called Arab–Afghans had soon become widely unpopular for being impostors who interfered where they were not welcome, as well as for their numerous atrocities, and their wanting to get their grubby foreign hands on the people's souls. When a democratic government was set up, the Wahhabis and their cohorts were on the way out, but not before they had, with the blessing of the world's most wanted man, practised mass genocide on Persian-speaking Hazaras, ethnically cleansing them for two whole days, needlessly murdering defenceless civilians, including women and children, before killing nine Iranian diplomats and almost starting a war with Iran.

For this war crime alone, the Arab–Afghans and the world's most wanted man ought to have been put on trial in The Hague. But, incredibly, nobody seemed to appreciate that they had settled an old score with the Persian-speaking members of their own religion. These were Persian-speaking groups of whom they had never approved; in fact, they hated the Iranian members of their religion almost as much as they hated the Americans and Russians.

Meanwhile, in the desert kingdom, the king and the royal family continued to coexist with the Wahhabis, even though observers said that this could lead to their ruin, in the event of the Americans deciding that enough was enough, and going to the root cause of the problem – namely, identifying the desert land where the Wahhabis first made their bargain with the founding king who sold his and his country's soul to them.

20

In The Eye Of
The Storm

Expatriates in Saudi Arabia used to say – back in the 1970s
– that the Saudi government would never allow British,
European or American citizens to be executed in the desert
kingdom. That's what most expatriates and many of their Saudi
Arabian friends said. That's what they thought.

It was extremely wishful thinking, of course (calculated to
calm the nerves and keep everyone happy), but it was
commonly believed that the Saudis' barbaric customs and
medieval laws were strictly reserved for Muslims, and could
never be applied to Western visitors from a modern world that
lived by much more modern laws.

Many Saudi Arabians encouraged their Western guests to
believe this nonsense. It's an 'understanding', the expatriates
argued, between them and us, a 'gentleman's agreement'
that the Saudis would 'never decapitate a Westerner, or stone
a Western woman to death. They would deport Westerners

rather than butcher them in the name of their medieval justice.'

'Nonsense,' I said, 'you can't be serious. Don't be so racist. Of course they would not make an exception of us. Why should they? What's so special about us? Why should the desert kingdom have one law for itself and another for us, as if to suggest that we are in some way superior and above it all? Get real. Of course they would execute and stone Westerners to death if they thought fit. They are already flogging and torturing some Westerners, so why stop there? Many Arabians would dearly love to see Western and wicked Christian heads roll in 'Chop Square'. They enjoy the spectacle of Muslim heads on the roll, so why would they not get an extra kick out of seeing white Christian heads severed from their bodies?'

'They never would,' came the insistent head-in-the-sand reply. 'It would cause too much of a stink in the Western world – too much of a diplomatic incident – for the Saudis to do such a horrendous thing to Westerners. They are highly polished gentlemen, the rulers of this country. They have been educated in Britain and America and are truly civilised. They actually like us and, what is more, they need our weaponry and arms in return for their oil, if they are to stay in power. They need our military protection. Everybody knows that it's a marriage of convenience between them and us, and the desert kingdom is an oil-rich playground for an Arabian royal family that happens to be on our side.'

'In your dreams,' I said, 'just you wait and see. Western heads will roll here, sooner or later, and there will come a time when the Saudis will feel that they do not need our military protection any more, because, with our help, they are rapidly becoming militarily so much stronger on their own account.'

That was in the 1970s.

We are now in the year 2003 and times are changing dramatically.

The Saudi Government is beginning to think that it might be better if the United States of America withdrew its 5,000 troops from the desert kingdom where an increasing number of anti-Americans are accusing the US military of, among other things, polluting holy Muslim air. And a handful of British expatriates have been thrown behind bars and mysteriously put on trial for a murder for which there is precious little known or examinable evidence, and for which a lot of people say that they have been falsely accused and framed. Should these expatriates – who are reportedly being treated like dogs by their jailers – be found guilty of murder in some weird and mysterious way under Saudi law then they are liable to be executed in accordance with that law.

But surely this could never happen, asks an English television interviewer of the new millennium, in an interview in London with the desert kingdom's ambassador there, who is a high-ranking prince, a senior member of the Saudi royal family.

The Saudi Ambassador tells him frankly that 'if found guilty of murder' they will 'of course, be executed'.

Stunned silence. This in unthinkable. Unspeakable!

But isn't it the case that those being accused of murder are being tortured in desert kingdom jails to make them confess to crimes they haven't committed?

'If someone has committed torture,' says the Ambassador demurely, 'he will be punished for it.'

He's a nice guy, the Saudi ambassador, a perfect gent, and so smartly clad in a finely tailored Western suit. You could introduce him to your grandmother. The Ambassador comes over as the sort you can trust when he gives you his word. He is top drawer, cut glass, polite, smooth talking, calm, suave and looking as though butter wouldn't melt in his mouth. The state-employed torturers in his country, if found guilty, will be punished, just as the British expatriates, if found guilty, will be executed. He gives us his word for it. Justice will be done (not that it will be seen to be done, but no matter, it will be done for all that, trust him).

Well, fair's fair, so perhaps we are approaching a time when the first Western heads will roll – when, shock horror, the unbelievable will happen. Of course, it's still a close run thing, the British expatriates may yet escape with their lives before this carefully orchestrated drama is over, so fingers crossed. But, on the other hand, they may not, and there can be no doubt that the Saudis are sending us a powerful message in their theatrical manner – sending their fanatics at home a message – which is, don't run away with the idea that we make exceptions for Western expatriates in our country, because we do not.

It's not only the Americans who need to get real in the Arab world and understand what they have got themselves into. It's the British and Europeans as well. We are all at risk and in the same boat. Nor is it just a matter of decapitated Western heads that may possibly be rolling in the desert kingdom in the near or foreseeable future. Robert Dent, a British white-collar worker in his thirties, who had been working there for ten years, was shot to death in his car at some traffic lights in early 2003 – presumably for being white, Western, unwelcome and working for BAE systems in Riyadh – presumably by an Al-Qaeda terrorist who wants to rid his country of Westerners and overthrow the puppet royal family whose strings are pulled by the West.

Western expatriates in the desert kingdom today can expect

far less justice than asylum seekers in Britain and Continental Europe, and their embassies should tell them so. And these expatriates can certainly expect to be executed if they don't watch out. They are in an extremely dangerous position, even though the desert kingdom is not, as yet, at war.

The Saudi Ambassador in London does not deny that his Government has rounded up 250 Al-Qaeda suspects and charged 90 of them. He concedes this on British television before millions of viewers and he describes Osama bin Laden, whom he has met, as 'the most horrendous terrorist in modern history'.

But who is to blame for spawning this horrendous terrorist? Bin Laden is from a highly privileged Saudi family in the desert kingdom, where he learned his religion and his race hate, and where he was once financed and fully supported by the Saudi and US Governments, was he not?

The Ambassador says that he thinks that Osama is to blame, not anyone else, because it is he who has turned himself into a terrorist, and what is more the ambassador believes that Osama is still alive 'probably in Pakistan, next to the Afghan border'. The Ambassador – a Muslim and an Arab – does not say that he thinks the injustice done to the Palestinians by Israel and the US is to blame, or that Western influences in his ancient country are to blame. He says that Osama is the only one to blame.

This is all a far cry from the 1970s when it seemed that nobody was to blame for anything and Western expatriates pouring into the kingdom had one thought only – to make hay while the sun shines.

But these days the Saudi royal family is decidedly worried that the kingdom of Saudi Arabia could become 'Osama Arabia' if enough of its citizens were to go over to Al-Qaeda. So who is to say that it will not falsely accuse and behead a few Westerners in future – like human sacrifices – if that's what it takes to keep its fanatics on side and save its own highly polished skin? Who is to say that it will not ask the US to withdraw its troops in order to keep its US-hating Saudis sweet (knowing perfectly well that the US will be back in double-quick time should the Saudis find that they cannot cope without them)? Who is to say that some of the desert kingdom's policies will not become more populist in future?

Is this a dagger I see before me?

Talk about all the perfumes of Arabia!

But the thing to remember is this: the Saudi royal family and its government are in the eye of the storm – as are the helpless British expatriates accused, almost certainly falsely, of murder – and that storm, which originally came from Saddam Hussein back in the 1990s, is now coming from Osama bin Laden in the new millennium. And it's all motivated by greed, megalomania and power politics under the guise of ideology and moral concern (it's not only the Americans who want the oil and are the hypocrites – by no means!)

Coming from Osama, this storm is *much* closer to home than previous storms, and like most sandstorms it is one in which it is virtually impossible to see the way ahead in this vicious circle of dark intrigue, foul conspiracy and deeply flawed human nature in the Arab and Western worlds today.

21

An Invitation to a Friend

'Come and live with us and put all your sins under our safekeeping. You will be as safe as houses ... or perhaps we should say tents.'

'No, let's talk of houses. I hate tents.'

'We are actually talking about desert palaces. Come into a rich and easy retirement and let us protect you. All your personal needs will be catered for. You will want for nothing. Come here and prepare to meet your maker while there is still time. Come and prepare your mind by contemplating the error of your ways and repenting at leisure. Come and be forgiven.'

'But I have done nothing wrong!'

'So much the better. But you must come here if you wish to survive. You've had a good run for your money, so get out now while you still can, and enjoy an early retirement. Enjoy what is left of your life. Come and learn how to be – if not a reformed character, since you have done nothing wrong – then a new man in a place in the sun where the Americans will leave you alone at last and the world will eventually forget you, as we draw a veil over you and your past. As you know, that is how we do things here. We draw a veil over everything.'

'It's a very persuasive offer, but how do I know that I can trust your Government?'

'Idi Amin trusted us and he is still alive and well to tell the tale, living in style in our holy land. His alleged crimes were at least as bad as yours. Remember all those body parts in his refrigerator after he chopped up his victim's body like a piece of meat? Remember how he outraged the Americans and the Western world? He was the world's most wanted man when he first came here. Now he is long forgotten and hardly missed by the outside world. We kept our word to him and we would certainly keep it to you too, for you are family, a fellow Arab and a blood brother. Even though you dropped some of your scud missiles on us during the previous war, we shall forgive you if you come here. I expect it was an accident anyway.'

'But Idi Amin did not find it necessary to slaughter fellow Arabs and Kurds, as I have, and he has not dealt in biological weapons of mass destruction.'

'No matter. Your crimes will soon be forgotten as they disappear into the mists of time. And do not forget, many of your biological and other weapons have served the Muslim and Arab cause well. Where would Al-Qaeda and other terror groups be without your weapons, which were always there when they needed them? Most Arabs have admired the way you have stood up to the West and waged war on those despised Iranians, who call themselves Muslims, but are not Arabs or even Sunis. You are in the same boat as Idi and, since we have kept him afloat on an ocean of sand all these years, we can certainly come to your rescue as well.'

'But are you sure that Idi is still alive?'

'Of course. You don't think that we have quietly murdered him, do you?'

'Why not? Such things happen in this part of the world. Maybe you did it quietly as a service to the Americans. Maybe you plan to do the same to me as a further service to them.'

'Oh, come now. Would you like to meet with Idi and hear what he has to say about his exile here? Then you can judge for yourself. You will find that he is happy these days. Grateful, too.'

'Yes, please do arrange a meeting. Let me hear it from the horse's mouth.'

'He wised up, you see, and you must do that, too. Wise up and come here and be his neighbour.'

'As an exiled leader, what would my status be exactly?'

'Well, of course, you could not travel outside the kingdom, so we would have to relieve you of your passport for the duration of your stay. But you could always have it back should you change your mind and decide to leave us in the fullness of time. But you would be able to afford to live in a luxurious palace here and have as much illegal booze and as many servants as you need. And you would not be short of female company, because we have brothels and harems aplenty here, and there is plenty of white female flesh on offer, in addition to the usual Arabian flesh. In addition to any female company of your own that you may wish to bring with you, you would not be short of sex and, as you know, we also have a ready supply of houseboys, should you wish to vary your sexual tastes. You really would want for absolutely nothing, and you would doubtless be discreetly invited to join our royal hunting parties from time to time.'

'But exile is such a serious step for any leader to take.'

'It's better than sitting in Baghdad and getting your head blown off by the Americans.'

'But I may escape from them and live to fight another day.'

'You may indeed. But they will definitely replace you and your Government this time, with another that is more to their liking, and most of your people will soon forget you. You will be on the run and perhaps getting nowhere fast. Better by far to retire gracefully and with dignity, by coming here, while there is still time. Deny the Americans their opportunity to have your head, or to humiliate you by driving you out, and perhaps turning your people against you. Your people will thank you, if you step down now, in order to avoid this war and the destruction of your country and its economy all over again and, who knows, your people may invite you back again – or allow you to quietly return, in the years ahead when the dust has settled? If you come now, with all your wealth intact still, you will be able to live very comfortably here.'

'But exile is such a lonely place, is it not?'

'Admittedly, it is quieter than Iraq here. But this is a good place to think about and change your life if you are in a mood to do so. You can visit the holy cities of Mecca and Medina as often as you like and we have some of the most learned *mullah*s in Islam to console and counsel you.'

'You do?'

'Of course! Why do you look so surprised?'

'I don't know. I expect that I never thought of that before.'

'Think of it now, my friend, and think hard and quickly, because you are running out of time.'

'But exile is such a punishment.'

'Believe me, it is the least harmful of the punishments that are coming in your direction. If you must think of it as a punishment, think of it as one of life's more kindly and temporary punishments, from which only your emotions will suffer, and not your precious body. At least you will save your skin whilst suffering emotionally to begin with – and perhaps psychologically, who can tell? – but, in due course, you will emerge the better for it, as Idi has done. Don't think of this place as hell on earth, but as a very convenient and entirely luxurious last resting place. Come here and go out in style. For Idi it has proved to be a forgiving place of correction to prepare him for the next world, to purge him of his former sins.'

'I cannot believe that he is still alive.'

'Do not be so suspicious. I will arrange for you to meet him.'

'And you truly believe that he has purged himself of his former sins?'

'Oh yes, he is a changed man now ... The Americans will not pursue you here. We have it on good authority from President Bush himself that you can mysteriously disappear off the face of the earth as far as he is concerned, as long as you are never heard of again. You can disappear into our protective custody, and he will be well pleased, for as long as our royal family are here to keep a watchful eye on you. I expect our royals will take you to their bosom. Bush really wants you to come here.'

'Ha! Bush. That swine! I spit on him. I spit on the United Snakes of America.'

'Yes, yes, quite so. But never mind him any more. Think now of your future safety. Think of saving your skin and the skins of your family before it is too late. Think of the great Arab family of which we are all members and such passionate blood brothers, for better or worse, and never forget that this is a family that looks after its own. Unlike the Christians and

Europeans, we know how to look after our own. Never forget that we are a brotherhood.'

'Including the sorely neglected Palestinians?'

'How can you ask such a thing? They are the poor relations, of course, but they are family for all that. All families have their rich and poor, good and bad members, but they still remain united as families.'

'It's a very generous and tempting offer that you are making. But why?'

'We do not want political and economic chaos in this part of the world, and we certainly do not want an expanded American presence either in our country or on our doorstep. We have told the Americans, with whom we have had a strong relationship for 60 years, that we are prepared to do whatever it takes to prevent a war, and to safeguard the Iraqi people, even if that means forgiving you for threatening us back in the 1990s. And, as you know, we Arabs believe that our enemy's enemy is our friend, so now that Osama has become our enemy these days – as he is yours – it is now possible for you to become our friend. We do not believe that you, or anyone, can stand up to the US, so a war between you and them would be no contest, in our opinion, and it would only serve to rock our boat at present, and this is not good. It's better for us all if you retire now. You would feel at home here. Our human rights record is as appalling as yours. You would like the atmosphere here.'

'But why hasn't your country joined me in my fight against the Americans?'

'It is not possible. We are all realists here. There is too much wealth and power at stake. It is our destiny to go along with the Americans and we are very embarrassed that so many of the September 11th terrorists had desert kingdom passports. As you know, we have had a special relationship with the US for such a long time and it is most rewarding and suits us very well. We think you have been terribly misguided to inflame them the way you have. As it happens, we like their fat-cat mentality and their power politics in this part of the world, which suits our purpose very well. They are the lesser of several evils, as far as we are concerned, so we do not wish to cross them and their Western allies. They have given us their word that they will not harm you or us if you come here. Probably, they will want you to slip through the back door, without letting the world know that you are here. So you will have to disappear. That's how Idi did it. If it is not known that you are here, we shall not be asked by the Americans to hand you over to them because, in the eyes of the world, they will have no reason to suspect that you are here. They will turn a blind eye and pretend that they do not know. So they will not lose face, which is very important. There is an MP in Britain who wants you indicted as a war criminal, I believe.'

'I spit on such MPs. But I don't like the idea of hiding behind anyone's skirts.'

'I can understand that, but you have no choice, you really don't. You are fast running out of options and we have wide skirts. The best on offer.'

'If I do come here, what about that bastard Osama?'

'What about him?'

'He hates my guts. He thinks me too secular.'

'Don't worry about him. He hates everyone's guts. I am not sure that he likes himself very much. For as long as he is hating American and Christian guts in different parts of the world, that suits us just fine, because he won't have time for hating you and the rest of us who deplore his fanaticism. He won't be able to rattle our cage. Don't forget, you will be allowed to bring your own bodyguards and henchmen with you, and to arm yourselves within certain limits. So I don't think that Osama will bother you. We, too, shall protect you.'

'Is Osama here already?'

'I don't think so.'

'You don't think so? You mean to say that you don't know?'

'I don't have to tell you, of all people, that it's hard to be sure of anything in this country. You understand how things are in this part of the world. But as far as we can tell, he is not here. We cannot say for certain, because he has friends and supporters who could no doubt smuggle him in and hide him away under our noses, but we keep an ever-watchful eye on all parts of the kingdom, and we are of the opinion that he is in Pakistan, Yemen or somewhere like that – perhaps even in your country, in the north, where he has a few terrorist friends, I believe?'

'I don't know where the hell he is, but I don't want him anywhere near me.'

'Fear not, he will not trouble you here, should you decide to come. Al-Qaeda is active in this country, but we are fighting them.'

'If I come, shall I be required to pray five times a day? Don't forget that I am a secularist.'

'Not at all. Inside the high walls of your own palace you can do what you like. But don't say "if I come", talk instead of when you will come.'

'I will think very seriously about it and I thank you kindly for your invitation.'

'Think of it as an invitation to a friend in his hour of need.'

'An invitation to two friends, surely? To me and to your American friend whom you have invited to let you intervene in this way?'

'Yes, a dual-purpose invitation. We in the desert kingdom are not as stupid as some people seem to think. We invite you to come here for the greater good and stability of the region. And we invite our American friend to consent to this. It is the Arab way.'

'I will think on it.'

'But don't take too long to make up your mind, because, I repeat, you must decide quite soon now.'

'First I must meet with Idi Amin, to make sure that he is, as you say, still alive and well to tell the tale.'

'Leave it with me.'

22

DEFENSIVE
IMPERIALISM

This is a story of defensive imperialism, Saudi style. Not many people know what defensive imperialism means.

Not in the Arab world or, indeed, the world at large, but in the desert kingdom of Saudi Arabia – which has some 5,000 US troops on its shores and is, arguably, the place where defensive imperialism has been invented and thoroughly tested – most educated people know exactly what it means, and it is this that has got up Al-Qaeda's nose.

And what it means is this: an imperial power will, when called upon to do so, act in the defensive interests of another weaker power in order to protect it and its resources from invasion, terrorism or misrule. It follows that a smaller power must have some resources that are worth protecting and that it gets on reasonably or very well with the imperial power in question (unless the weaker power in question is the victim of such an ugly crime against humanity that is so offensive to the conscience of the civilised world that the only thing that matters is to do the right thing, regardless of a smaller power's resources, or how well it happens to get on with its protectors!)

Considering the role of the United States in Saudi Arabia, it is certainly possible to argue that it is in the desert kingdom where defensive imperialism has been invented ahead of other countries. An imperial power is, by definition, one that extends its political clout and commercial interests by having a presence in another country, which is why it is there in the first place. And defensive imperialism is, by definition, a voluntary and co-operative form of imperialism that can be justified on grounds of military defence. It is a new form of imperialism not, as yet, terribly well known, or openly acknowledged in diplomatic and other circles (probably because it smacks too much of the white man's burden).

But whilst this new form of imperialism is voluntary, it is still imperialism for all that – that is to say the dependency of a smaller country on a much larger one, the latter of which will establish and increase its influence, diplomacy and perhaps trade as a result of the protection that it is providing, and maybe with a view to getting the lion's share of the richest pickings.

There are, of course, a lot of anti-imperialists and former colonial countries throughout the world to whom the word imperialism is anathema and, understandably, these countries cannot stand the idea of a return to any type of imperialism in any shape or form (which is why, when it happens in Saudi Arabia, or elsewhere, it may very well be denied that it is happening, on account of its being an extremely sensitive and universally unpopular issue).

Even so, it cannot be denied that there are countries in this big bad world that are beginning to wonder if imperialism isn't the lesser of evils, so it may very well emerge as a new political animal in the twenty-first century. If so, it will show its hand not as once it did in the distant past – when unashamed empire builders flagrantly imposed their will – but as in a modern and enlightened world where a kid-gloved imperial power is invited, with a hand shake, and as a welcome guest that is much more co-operative and better behaved than before (but still not without the inevitable trappings of the old imperialism).

So history will be repeating itself and the imperialism on offer will come with the usual strings attached, albeit voluntary, rather than enforced.

But, as more and more weak countries are threatened and perhaps taken over by small, illegitimate and deeply immature and irresponsible terrorist groups and rogue states – who are these days increasingly a law unto themselves – defensive imperialism may prove to be the only answer in some parts of the world where there are obvious baddies – absolute stinkers – who are suddenly in a powerful position to have their wicked way with relatively harmless goodies (as we have seen in Afghanistan, Kuwait, the Balkans and elsewhere).

And these baddies, few in number, are suddenly in a powerful position to unseat legitimate governments in small countries who can no longer stand up to them – and even to punish and disrupt large countries to which they object for whatever reason – thanks to the uncontrolled spread of modern technology and weapons of mass destruction, including biological weapons (a handful of terrorists can cripple the economies of large countries in the new millennium and bring us all down).

For all of the seriously good things that modern science has achieved for the human race, it has also achieved enough destructive and seriously bad things to wipe out the good at a single stroke, so the world's scientists, and not just its politicians, have a lot to answer for, and not least their lack of conscience and foresight. They have let the rats out of the sewer in many parts of the world, enabling them to become far too big for their boots, and it is for this reason that we may now have no choice but to resort to some defensive imperialism to prevent global anarchy.

The reason why defensive imperialism is well understood in Saudi Arabia and the Gulf States is because we have seen, in recent times, Saddam Hussein's unprovoked invasion of Kuwait in order to pinch its oil, his mass genocide of the Marsh Arabs, his partial genocide of the Kurds and his slaughter of millions of his own people, not to mention the ever present threat of an invasion of Saudi Arabia by Saddam. We have seen all these things, in addition to the continuing impotence and lack of resolve of a squeamish and flaky United Nations, with its 1,001 windbags, to do anything about them (or, indeed, the plight of the Palestinians).

And the reason why the US suddenly wants to put a stop to these things, after procrastinating for far too long, is because they had got out of hand, not only with Saddam – who threatened to become an even greater threat had he built himself some atom bombs – but with many others as well, some of whom the US fears that Saddam has been supporting in one way or another. Since September 11th the US has woken up and is predictably scared, and Saddam has become the first and most obvious of an increasing number of perfectly legitimate and long-overdue targets in different parts of the world. And the reason why the French, Germans and others of their persuasion have not wanted to grasp the nettle in Iraq is because they have been running scared, hoping that the Arab terrorists who already have them in their sights will leave them alone if they take no action (but not realising that terrorists have never respected surrender monkeys, or shown any mercy to those who beg for it). They have also had significant commerce interests in Iraq.

Add to this catalogue of bullying and international law-breaking by Saddam, that is so uncomfortably close to Saudi Arabia's borders, the equally chilling internal threat of Al-Qaeda inside the desert kingdom, seeking to overthrow the Saudi royal family and its Government, and it is not difficult to understand the new appeal of defensive imperialism to Saudi Arabia, Kuwait and other such countries. One can immediately see the sense of it. When it came to trusting either to the sanity and restraint of a tyrannical dictator and mad war criminal, such as Saddam Hussein, or to US defensive imperialism, there was no contest in many if not most Saudi minds – they will volunteer for US imperialism any day of the week (as would some other Arab states if the truth were known).

In other parts of the world, too, we may see more defensive imperialism in future, as very small terrorist groups and rogue states become intolerable, and as leaders such as Robert Mugabe start pursuing internationally unacceptable policies. (When Mugabe turned over the white farms to ordinary blacks with no basic education, let alone any experience of farming, we were treated to the hideous spectacle of black thugs who were so low on the human scale that they immediately stoned the farm animals to death for their own pointless amusement, tethering them to stakes in the ground and hurling rocks and stones at them in a sick and mindless sporting activity – we also saw some white farmers and their workers needlessly murdered and beaten to a pulp.)

There can be no doubt that there are many in Zimbabwe today who would wish for some defensive imperialism from Britain.

Of course, there is no defensive imperialism in Africa, but in the desert kingdom of Saudi Arabia it is alive and well, and as the world becomes much more of a jungle in the years ahead – in which the vicious law of the jungle increasingly prevails – then we may have to look to defensive imperialism, as the Saudis have done, if we are to save the civilised world from the barbarians at the gate.

It doesn't follow from this that today's imperialists will be out to steal the resources of those countries that volunteer for the new-fangled imperialism on offer. The US did not steal Iraq's or Kuwait's oil (when it rescued the latter from the former during the Gulf War back in the 1990s) and there is no reason to believe that it is interested in stealing Iraq's oil today. It is not the US that has a record of daylight robbery in different parts of the globe. But the US is interested in saving the free market and preventing Iraq becoming an atomic power and supplying US-hating terrorist groups with weaponry, as Saddam has almost certainly been doing in Northern Iraq where insiders know perfectly well that Al-Qaeda has a presence and that its terrorists – who cannot be bothered to speak either Iraqi or Kurdish and care little for their respective customs or cultures – have already terrorised Iraqis and repeatedly murdered Kurds whose faces do not fit.

No doubt the Kurds could do with some defensive imperialism themselves but, as things stand, it doesn't look as though they are going to get any. They don't have any oil or petro-dollars, like the Saudis and Kuwaitis, both of whom have volunteered for defensive imperialism, not that either of them will ever admit it in so many words.

Imperialism?

Goodness me, what a retrograde step that would be. Such backward thinking. Perish the thought!

23

AN EXTRACT FROM
MY DIARY

MONDAY

Made the mistake of going out without my passport today.
Thought nothing of it until I saw an Arabian policeman coming
in my direction, with the intention of doing a stop and search,
as I crossed the road outside the supermarket. They don't muck
around, these policemen, and they think nothing of going
through your pockets if you don't immediately produce your
passport upon demand. I expect they know that expatriates
sometimes forget to take their passports with them when they
go out. So we are fair game, in a way, under the law. But what a
stupid law it is. Do they seriously believe that expatriate
residents are spies from abroad? Getting in and out of this
country is like breaking into Fort Knox or escaping from a
prison – in view of the entrance and exit visas – so what's with
this stop-and-search passport business? I expect that the police

just like an excuse to harass white skins. They don't seem to like us very much, most of them. Mind you, the situation is not much better for brown skins either, because the police regularly ask them if they are Muslims, and then cheerfully slap their faces if the answer is no, as if to suggest that it is very remiss of them to have joined the wrong religion! Even the Arabian taxi-drivers take a page out of the police's book and slap their passengers' brown faces for having forgotten to do the decent thing and become a Muslim. But it's the first time that I have forgotten to take my passport with me. Others forget theirs and never seem to get stopped, yet as soon as I do it, I get caught first time. Just my luck.

I was taken to the police station, of course, to give an account of myself, and they eventually released me, after a tedious couple of hours' interrogation, during which time they phoned my office and satisfied themselves that I was an OK person. By the time I got back to the supermarket, it was closed for prayers! I should have remembered that there are always plenty of police in evidence in and outside the supermarket, on account of it being the only place where Arabian women are allowed to drop their veils, inside the store, in order to do their shopping and to look face to face at strange men, behind the counters and along the aisles. I expect the police hang out there, not just to prevent any men going wild with lust when they see a female face in public, but also to have a good look themselves. How weird. The so-called religious police go into the store to make sure that the unveiled women are behaving themselves, while the other police who walk the beat stay outside.

It's such a drag having to remember to take your passport with you wherever you go – to the office, local shops, restaurants and so on – but I am usually pretty good at disciplining myself and remembering these things. Some white women I know always forget to put their passports in to their handbags, and the police just love detaining them, for obvious reasons.

I have been in this country for almost 12 months now and have a couple of remaining months to go. I have never before forgotten to carry my passport with me. Let's hope I don't forget it again.

Nothing much else happened today. Time crawls so slowly here, like a snail suffering from heat exhaustion. One needs a lot of inner resource and strength of character to put up with the loneliness, boredom and culture clash here. And it helps a lot if you like your own company and can somehow fill the emptiness that is this nowhere-to-go and nothing-to-do country, in which do-nothing people are similarly in danger of becoming nothing, nothing at all. Good job I brought plenty of novels and classical music cassettes with me.

TUESDAY

People who survive here and stay for the duration say that it's the first three months that count. They reckon that, if you can get your head round three months of the garbage that is thrown at you, your adjustment can last for as long as you like. Three months is the acid test. It's as long as it takes to push someone from the outside world to the limit. Impatient Australian businessmen have a tendency to blow their tops and storm off in a matter of days. This is certainly a place to try your patience. One of our Indian journalists from Britain became so hyper that he had to be stretchered out of here inside the first three months and put on a plane back to Britain.

Another boring day, not least on account of Ramadan, during which non-Muslims are required to observe the religious ban on daytime eating in public and work places. I have devised a cunning plan to overcome this problem, which has worked well today, so let's hope it continues to do so. I got the idea of hard boiling some eggs, shelling them and then smuggling them into the office in my briefcase, which I keep at my feet under my desk, with the case open. When the religious police who patrol the office were looking the other way, I managed to pop the occasional egg into my mouth unobserved and chew it up quickly! While I doubt that it is doing my digestion much good – popping eggs into my mouth like grapes and quickly swallowing them – it is keeping my stomach together during the day, without anyone being any the wiser that at least one non-Muslim is managing to eat his fill during Ramadan. I have become a secret hard-boiled-egg-eater! Sometimes, when others look in my direction, or ask me a question, I nod or shake my head accordingly, as I remain tight-lipped until my mouth is empty. Once or twice I have received strange looks, but I don't think that anyone suspects what I am up to. The Arabians are not very observant because, having been up all night feeding their faces, to make up for their lack of food during the day, they are dead tired, so they collapse in their chairs, snoring their sleepy way through working hours, with their heads on their arms, resting on their desks. It's OK for them, because they eat into the night – partying all night long, I hear – and then sleep instead of doing any work the following day. But it's hard and unfair on the expats, because they have not been eating all night and they are weakened by a serious lack of food during the day, but must carry on working regardless, and they are having to work harder than usual in order to make up for the lack of Muslim manpower during working hours.

This really is an impossible country for non-Muslims. On the other hand, we all get paid much more than we deserve, and there is no tax to pay, so we shouldn't complain too much. If we don't like it, we can always do the other thing. Not that getting out of this country is easy. Without the Government issuing an exit visa, nobody is going anywhere, and it takes several weeks to get an exit visa approved and processed. The authorities really can keep people here for as long as they wish, if they are in a mood to do so. I wonder if my hard-boiled-egg trick will work tomorrow and for the rest of Ramadan. People are already remarking on how I seem to be able to survive in the absence of food, without complaint or any slackening of my work performance. I would let other expats into my secret, but the trouble is that some of them have big mouths and gossip far too much. If word got out what I was up to, the religious police would doubtless be down on me like a ton of bricks, searching my briefcase and hauling me off to the police station again. Think I'll keep my secret vice to myself, for fear of indiscreet colleagues letting the cat out of the bag.

Got home and was really thirsty after eating so many dry eggs, so I drank gallons of water in the absence of booze (I must get round to the British Embassy bar for some more gin and tonic at the first opportunity). Hard-boiled is what I am becoming here, which is perhaps no bad thing in the circumstances.

WEDNESDAY

The hard-boiled eggs are making me constipated! So I am now having to eat plenty of chillies in the evenings.

I could not get a gin and tonic at the British Embassy's illegal bar today, or any other kind of black-market booze for that matter. This is because the Embassy's regular monthly consignment of hooch has not been smuggled into the desert kingdom this month, so the bar is dry.

The word is that the consignment has gone missing because, when it arrived in the docks in a container – suitably disguised as a 'piano', according to the label on the container – there was a minor catastrophe. The inexperienced Arabian crane operator, who was hoisting the cargo off the ship, managed to lose grip of it, so that it came crashing down to the ground and cracked open, spilling whisky over the quayside for all to see. Horror of horrors.

This was very embarrassing and potentially quite dangerous in a fanatical country in which the sinful consumption of alcohol is illegal and its ordinary people – including crane operators, dockers and customs officers – are severely punished for drinking black-market hooch.

So, when the British Embassy got a call from Arabian Customs, saying that its piano was leaking, and could not be delivered without the customs men opening the container up, to see what had gone wrong inside and how the contents could be rescued, the British Ambassador had a blue fit. It's one thing for Arabians and expatriate workers to be punished when they are caught brewing or consuming illegal booze. But it's quite another matter for a foreign embassy and its staff to be caught out regularly importing tons of forbidden hooch, and with the sly connivance of the desert kingdom's government and royal family, who obligingly look the other way when diplomats are thirsty, telling their law-makers that foreign diplomats are a special case. Such appalling double standards might cause a revolution on the streets one of these days.

For this reason, the British ambassador – whose embassy ought to be chock full of pianos, on account of its theoretically receiving the delivery of one such musical instrument per month (in fact, there is only one broken-down old piano to be found at the embassy, gathering dust in a back room) – urgently dispatched his chargé d'affaires to the docks to see what could be done. When the poor man got there, a diplomatic incident was rapidly looming large, because a crowd had gathered and was sniffing the golden elixir leaking from the container, and dipping their fingers into it to see how it tasted. The quick-thinking chargé d'affaires – who is second only to the ambassador as a man who has gone into the world to lie for his country – declared in a very loud voice, 'this cannot be one of our pianos, because British pianos never leak. Send it back to London at once.'

As a result of which, the Embassy bar will remain dry now for a whole month, until the next assignment of musical booze.

What a drag. I must see if I can confirm this story.

THURSDAY

My bed collapsed last night while I was in the land of nod. I really wish I had stayed in the Omar Khyam hotel. This flat is crap. It's modern and clean enough, but too many things go wrong.

Workmanship is very dodgy here – much worse than at home – and the man who constructed my bed ought to be given a public flogging. I joke, of course, but the authorities think nothing of flogging other wrong-doers, so why not add crap workmen to the mind-boggling list?

It usually takes a lot to wake me, but when the bed fell apart last night, I woke with a frightful start. It was, to say the least, very alarming. To begin with, I thought I was having a nightmare, in which the whole world was falling apart and crashing round my ears. But when I discovered that it was only the bed that had fallen apart, beneath my sleeping body, I was momentarily relieved. *But only momentarily*, because I soon realised that I wouldn't be getting any more sleep for the rest of the night, and this made me angry, as well as tired. Well, how many people like to have their sleep disturbed in such a way, or to have a bed to reconstruct and hammer together in the middle of the night, when all they want to do is get their head down?

It took me at least an hour to discover that the bed would not fit back together again, so I decided to leave it until the crack of dawn, when I would ring the local carpenter and get him out of his bed, to see how he felt about that. Then I thought, to hell with the dawn, I'll ring the bloody man now to teach him a lesson.

When I did so, he was not amused, so I managed to make my point. But he put the phone down on me, saying I should wait until morning, after he had enjoyed a good night's sleep. When morning came, I told him that I wanted my money back, but he reckoned that he had already spent it – he is certainly not a rich man – and he suggested that a quick repair would do the trick. I hope so, because it's no fun being woken up and losing sleep in such a way. No sign of him today.

In London, I could dine out on such tales. But here, nobody is particularly interested or concerned, because this country is so bizarre and such hard work that these things are unsurprising. They are commonplace and people just shrug their shoulders and say, 'So what, what else is new?' Nothing seems to move or trouble or impress or disturb anyone here. People are generally impassive and unamused by most things. Whether it's at a public beheading, or the stoning to death of an adulterous woman in public, they just shrug their shoulders and walk away (unless they are morbid enough to get off on such grisly events, as many are).

A good sense of humour comes in handy in the desert kingdom, in order to see the funny side of things that are decidedly unfunny, even if you must keep it to yourself.

FRIDAY

Bed fixed. So fingers crossed. Let's hope for some good sleep from here on, without any more rude interruptions.

A single drop of rain fell from the sky today and it landed on my nose. A single drop of rain! What good is that? Clearly, the rain needs to get its act together in this part of the world.

Sometimes a handful of drops fall into the desert sand and swiftly disappear. God knows where the drops come from, because the sky is generally cloudless and blue. Probably they are blown in from elsewhere, travelling light on the wings of a breeze. It's quite an event when a mysterious handful of raindrops falls from on high, with not a cloud in sight. But when a single drops falls, nobody notices, other than the confused person on whose nose or face it lands.

The stars are so bright tonight, as I write these thoughts at the end of the day. They are always so clear and bright in the desert kingdom, but more so than usual tonight, or so it seems. They hang low in the night sky here, clear and bright in the darkness, smiling and happy. Probably they are happy because the scorching sun is no longer blistering and blinding all before it – because the suffocating heat has expired and one can breathe freely at last in the cool of night. They are icy cool, these beautiful stars, glacial and refreshing, sparkling like diamonds up there in the low-lying sky, which is otherwise so cruelly ravaged and savaged by a merciless and angry sun that burns all moisture and coolness out of it, fries all clouds on sight. Even the sky is a hard-boiled egg here. At the end of the oh-so-hot-and-tiring day, the night sky finally emerges, cool as a cucumber and all triumphant in the absence of the desert sun and its blue sky exploding with heat.

These dazzling stars are celebratory and in party mood. But they are not reflective of the mood of this place.

For the most part, one travels backwards in time here, not forwards. OK, so the country is being dragged, kicking and screaming, into the modern world, which is painted on like a cosmetic. But despite modernity, the kingdom's heart is actually going the other way. There is two-way traffic, but most of it, under the skin, is going backwards in time. As for these calming and graceful night stars, they are not going anywhere, and they look as though they have been here for ever, in their place of grace and serenity up there in the sky. They are comforting and healing, reassuring even, as they shine gently, unlike the sun, into the face of man, uplifting the human spirit, and keeping their cool in such a fiercely hot place, the temperature of which regularly climbs to 120 degrees in the shade. The stars, too, are part of the illusion and delusion, no doubt.

SATURDAY

Have been invited to *yet another* barbecue, but I cannot stand the usual expatriate tittle-tattle and gossip. Not exactly a meeting of seminal thinkers. More a case of empty-headed wankers.

Talking of wankers, there is always the all-male beach, of course, from which *all women* are banned. But what a pain that is, with not a woman in sight and so many of the men being homosexuals on the pull, particularly the Arabians who are always chatting up white flesh and trying to pick it up, discreetly of course. No, I would *not* like to come back to your place, thank you very much.

All-male beaches indeed! What a dumb idea, segregating men from women in this way, locking them into separate enclaves, so that the opposite sexes cannot even have a glimpse of each other, let alone get at one another. It stands to reason that such a beach will attract homosexuals like a magnet.

As for the all-female beach, that must be an even bigger drag for most women, because they are not allowed to wear bikinis or swimming costumes. They have to swim fully clothed in their *burka*s in case any prying male eyes should be spying on them from a distance, through binoculars. The women's beach must be a great place for lesbians, but it must be very boring for heterosexual women, just as it is for heterosexual men on the all-male beach. No, I think I'll give the men's beach a miss, as well as the barbecue. Of course, it's not just sexually segregated beaches here – it's cinemas, ice-cream parlours, workplaces and buses as well. Unashamed sexual apartheid looms large throughout the desert kingdom, where the fear of sex has to be seen to be believed.

I could always go for a swim in the hotel pool, where Western men and women are allowed to take a dip together, but the prices are inflated there, and it's dreadfully overcrowded, since there are too few public pools to go round. Perhaps I should get myself invited to a private villa with its own pool, but then again it's the tedious conversation. The people whose company I enjoy most are usually not at home at weekends, either because they are visiting other people, or because they are out in the desert on safari, which doesn't grab me either, because this is one roving reporter who has already spent too many of his working hours in the desert to want to return to it during his leisure time, thank you very much.

No, I think I'll stay in my apartment, read a novel or some poetry, and listen to classical music ... at least there's no ban on that, as yet. I shall be very glad when my time is up in this country. Can't wait to get back to London, never to return to this place that they call the 'land of the pure'.

SUNDAY

Received an unexpected invitation to a poolside Ramadan supper – in the villa of a rich oil sheikh who publishes Arabic newspapers. He phoned up to say that he has heard about my exploits in the desert, visiting people in remote villages in order to interview and write about them, and that he would like the opportunity of meeting me and discussing my impressions of life in the desert kingdom. Well, I thought, this kind of contact between Arabians and their expatriate guests needs to be encouraged. So I decided to go along, partly out of journalistic curiosity, but also because invitations from Arabian families are so rare that I took the view that perhaps they ought to be encouraged, in order to transcend the cultural and social barriers.

The sheikh agrees that much more contact between Arabians and their expatriate guests is needed and he seems to be very enlightened. He had no objection to my taking a dip with him, his wife and daughters in their pool, behind the high walls of his villa and beyond the prying eyes of neighbours and the outside world. His teenage daughter, who is quite pretty, is to go to Cambridge University, so her parents are very proud, of course, not least because most Arabians don't get the necessary grades at A-level to get into British universities. They finish up in inferior American ones instead, in California, and places like that.

The family turned out to be charming and interesting, and the sheikh is keen to syndicate my articles in his newspapers, so there will be some extra income for me that will be very welcome. He says that with his country's accursed press censorship – for which he actually apologised – he may have to edit some of my copy, but that won't bother me, since I shall not have the annoyance of reading his Arabic versions, after my work has been duplicated in this way. It's an English-language audience abroad that I'm writing for, so I'm not too fussed about what is published for Arabian readers here, since I am powerless to do anything about it or them.

MONDAY

As a result of meeting with my wealthy oil sheikh, I have now met the local mayor, who popped into my office to introduce himself, at the sheikh's suggestion. The mayor has told me of his ambitious project for naming the anonymous streets of this sprawling and dusty city, in which the roads have no names and the houses and buildings are numberless.

No wonder the mail hardly ever gets delivered on time or at all. Sometimes it arrives days or even weeks late. At other times it just mysteriously disappears after it has been posted. The word is that Arabian postmen become so frustrated trying to find their way around the anonymous streets – asking residents if they have heard of Mr and Mrs so and so, and whether they know where they live, in which turning and so on – that they sometimes lose the plot completely and just chuck the mail away out of exasperation, out in the desert where they cannot be seen, and where they imagine that the mail cannot be discovered.

There is always a backlog of undelivered mail after Ramadan, when the postal services are even slower and less reliable than usual, on account of tired postmen having been up all night feasting, and then sleeping in the following morning, instead of showing up at work. Come the end of Ramadan, the central post office just makes a mountainous pile of undelivered mail on some wasteland, before putting a light to it in one of the biggest bonfires of all time! Local company employees and residents are invited to scramble all over the paper mountain, to see if they can frantically discover any letters or parcels intended for them, before whatever remains of the unclaimed mail goes up in smoke. The post office reckons that it cannot be held responsible for the successful delivery of so much mail to vague addresses that cannot be found – such as Mr and Mrs X, somewhere along the third turning on the left, off the main road that runs between the airport and 'Chop Square'. Deliveries at any time of the year are almost impossible, but during and immediately after Ramadan, well, forget it. The daunting task is predictably hopeless. But the local mayor looks forward to a time when the mail will get cleared fast without the aid of a box of matches, even at the end of Ramadan, and delivered on time as a result of the streets being named and the buildings properly numbered after centuries of anonymity. He is an architect with an historic scheme for naming the city's streets, of which there are thousands, many centuries old.

In the old days, when everybody knew everyone else, and there was far less mail to deliver, it was not considered necessary to name streets and number their buildings, and people quite liked the mystery and privacy provided in an address-less kingdom. But with so much mail flooding into the kingdom from the outside world – and across the kingdom from one city, village and town to another – not to mention all the taxi drivers and foreign workers from out of town who are having to find their way around these days, the small-town mentality of yesteryear is supposed to be disappearing fast. And with the naming of streets and numbering of buildings comes the paving of the unpaved sidewalks as well.

In the absence of maps in the desert kingdom until the 1960s, the mayor and his staff used to walk round the streets to draw up the first-ever maps. But, now that the kingdom has struck it rich with oil, and is not short of petro-dollars, aerial surveys can be afforded, and this is making life a lot easier for the mayor and his ambitious plans.

TUESDAY

Now that I've finished my desert journeys and articles, I am spending more time in town, which makes a change from motoring for hundreds of kilometres in search of desert villages, where too many of the approach roads and motorways are littered with dead camels that get hit by heavy-duty trucks when the camels stray into the traffic. It also makes a change from having to take spare sets of tyres with you on long journeys, on which tyres generally explode in the excessive heat every 200 kilometres or so.

I shall never forget my journey to a remote desert village where I met a wrinkled old man who told me that he had fought with Lawrence of Arabia against the Turks.

Neither shall I forget a local sheikh who sent a gang of men to put my replacement tyres on my vehicle, while he entertained me to a meal, sitting cross-legged on the ground inside his tent. I made the mistake in the Village of the Wells of replying to him quite truthfully that I was 'not afraid', when he greeted me with the words, 'Don't be afraid, Englishman, we are all friends here.'

I ought to have said, 'Thank you,' or 'I'm very pleased to hear it,' or something like that, instead of which I made a terrible *faux pas*. What I'd meant was that I saw no reason to be afraid. But I gave him the impression that fear meant nothing to me, with or without his friendship, which is not true.

However, I did eventually manage to say the right thing to please him, when he said something in Arabic that I couldn't understand to one of his men, who quickly returned with a rifle that the sheikh proceeded to point at my head and, grinning, asked, 'Are you afraid now, Englishman?'

There was no doubt in my mind of my fear then, but again I wasn't prepared to admit it when I replied, 'Mind your own damn business.'

'Would you care to rephrase that, Englishman?' he said.

'My fear is my own business,' I replied, doing my best to keep a stiff upper lip, or something like that.

I was mightily relieved when he roared with laughter and declared, 'I like you, Englishman! You must eat with me,' as he put the rifle to one side. He was an interesting character, so rough and ready and wild, yet not uneducated, thanks to his father having paid for a tutor to come into the desert and teach him English, which he had mastered quite well. But I was a bit put off by having to share the same giant bowls of food with him and his retinue, all digging in with our dirty hands to the same piles of meat, rice and vegetables, belching and farting together in his tent. Talk about male bonding!

WEDNESDAY

Back at the office, I find myself peeing on the roof again with the rest of the editorial staff, when nature calls. More male bonding!

Because the stinking loos are so filthy in the dilapidated old building in which we find ourselves – with foul-smelling drains and burst pipes that spill urine all over the floor – the expatriates cannot bring themselves to use them, much to the amusement of the majority of the Arabians who think us such wimps for worrying about these things.

When nature calls, and it's a choice between a disgusting loo inside and an innocent and desperate pee outside, most of us are in favour of the roof any day of the week ... as are our Arabian female neighbours who, with welcoming smiles, have been keeping our dirty little secret for some months now.

This is a funny country. There are religious policemen virtually everywhere, spying on people for any whisper or sign of sexual immorality for which they can be warned, questioned, detained, arrested and perhaps punished, yet it doesn't occur to these zealots to take a look at the rooftops once in a while.

The alternative to peeing on the roof is walking or running at a fast pace for at least half-a-mile in the gruelling heat to a nearby hotel where they have perfectly clean and sweet-smelling loos. But who fancies doing that several times a day in this heat?

There are also rats in the office. They usually creep in late at night when we're typing by candlelight, on account of a power cut, and start to rummage around at our feet under our desks, in amongst the discarded pieces of paper, and in the waste paper baskets. We chase them out when we are not too busy, but when we're racing to meet a deadline, we generally ignore them.

Nobody has been bitten by a rat yet.

It puts one in mind of the Desert Rats, during World War II, who not only tamed the pesky little creatures and carried them with them as pets, but also named their regiment after them. But the desert rats were more like gerbils, whereas the desert kingdom's rats are much bigger and more bloated, and filthier and more germ-laden to boot, on account of the filthy loos where they hang out. They do not appeal as pets.

THURSDAY

Some people regard the desert kingdom as a sickening, horrifying, nightmare scenario, what with its rats, filthy loos, insanitary conditions, endless power cuts, extreme heat, lack of air-conditioning, unpaved sidewalks full of garbage, pot-holed roads, religious police, deep suspicion of foreigners, severe punishments, religious intolerance (including its ban on Christian worship and symbols), amazing prohibition on alcohol, public floggings and beheadings, the stoning to death of adulterous women and the amputation of thieves' hands, and so on. And it has to be said that such a bizarre and harsh place – which leaves so much to be desired – can be regarded as something of an uncomfortable and nerve-racking challenge, if not a punishment-posting for wrong-doers. It is true that one sometimes gets the feeling that one must have done something very wrong indeed to finish up here!

No doubt the garbage-strewn and unpaved sidewalks, pot-holed roads, insanitary conditions, power cuts, lack of air conditioning and filthy loos will soon be a thing of the past, eliminated by deodorised modernity. But one seriously doubts whether the rest of the nightmare will change for the better, or at all. Time will tell, but it would not surprise me if, come the new millennium, the medieval mind-set and customs here have not changed one jot.

But nightmare scenario notwithstanding, this is a good place for a relatively unknown journalist to make his name during an important moment in history, when he needs to do so, and when there is much to be learned and reported back to the outside world. Providing he can hang on to his wits, he can make his name because he has ready access to Arabian government ministers and members of royalty, all of whom are of global interest for the first time in their lives, because they hold the key to the oil weapon that has already resulted in a quadrupling of oil prices in the outside world where economies are being seriously challenged. He can also witness historical events that he could not witness elsewhere and get the *feel* of what they are actually like, simply by being here.

It's no longer any good for a journalist to sit in Cairo, dreading the day when, once a year, he must make an overdue visit to the sleepy old desert kingdom to see what, if anything, has been going on here. That's what my predecessor used to do. But it won't do from here on, because the 'sleepy old kingdom' is suddenly wide awake now, and the outside world is having to take note, whether it likes it or not, and it must take note, not from a distance, but from within the kingdom where it's all happening for the very first time. It's a matter of first come, first served, which is, of course, why I have come and decided to stay for as long as it takes. But I shall be glad to be on my way soon.

On Saturday I am to interview the government spokesman on oil prices for what will, no doubt, be a spirited discussion about 'Arabian oil prices, no holds barred'. I hear that he has strong views about this 'hot issue', having just got back from a tour of the United States where he has appeared on television screens and university campuses across the USA, defending the very steep oil price-hike of the Oil and Petroleum Exporting Countries (OPEC). He has had a rough ride in the States, and is reportedly fuming, so he would like to bend my ear to see if he cannot get a right of reply in *The Times*, which will, of course, give him a fair hearing.

FRIDAY

So glad Ramadan is soon to be over at last. We can all get back to eating properly again and doing a decent day's work.

The food in the desert kingdom is not much to write home about at the best of times. But, after a diet of hard-boiled eggs during the daytime prohibition, I can get back to my steaks and *shawama*s, or bananas and fruit juice. The camel meat in the *shawama*s is perfectly foul – spongy and tasteless. Much prefer to live on bananas and fruit juice most of the time. The bread is frequently stale and not very flavoursome, and most of the imported groceries are far too expensive. Anyway, part of my reason for being here is to make and save money, not to waste it on imported groceries that are seriously overpriced. As for the pubs with no beer and the hotels with no wines or spirits, well, life can be tough at 120 degrees in the shade. They have something called 'near beer'. It has a flavour of beer, but is without any alcoholic content whatsoever, and it costs a small fortune, as do £50 bottles of apple juice in restaurants – 'desert kingdom champagne' – and imported bottles of water at £20 per bottle.

The illegal hooch – *sadiki* – is cheap enough, but it is a rough sort of black-market gin that is not always safe to drink because some of it can damage your health, and you can be arrested if caught in possession of it. It can be refined and made palatable by use of cranberries and tonic water. But it's so much safer and better to drink at the British Embassy bar – or the American, Canadian, German, Austrian, Taiwanese and Korean Embassy bars, all of which are welcoming to me for some reason. I expect the embassies don't mind having me for drinks, so that they can bend my ear and gossip about each other, while seeing what they can learn from me about the competition. The Germans and Austrians are especially welcoming and pour some very passable dry white wines down my throat, whilst the Taiwanese Ambassador always wraps up a bottle of whisky in brown paper and hands it to me when I leave. He tells me, 'We Chinese are renowned for our patience, but this place is enough to try the patience of a saint, as you say in England.' The Indian and Pakistani Embassies are also welcoming, but they don't go in for as much alcohol, although their food is, of course, excellent.

Local Arabian cuisine is so dry and overcooked. Bloodless *halal* meat is drained of its taste and accompanied by mountains of dry rice loaded with dry nuts and sultanas. Chicken and fish are equally overcooked and tasteless. Sickly sweet Arabian tea really is dreadful, and there's not much coffee around. On the other hand, Arabian ice-cream is delicious, and there is some fruit, but too many sweet dates which are bad for the teeth. Street-corner kebabs are passable, but juicy American steaks, soft and tender, are a favourite, either at the US Embassy, or in US homes or company compounds. So, too, is Indian and Chinese food, if you can get an invite to dinner in these embassies or homes. Don't know much about English cooking because the Brits keep me at arm's length, as they suspect (correctly) that I write the 'Under the Wilton' column in *Private Eye*, and they don't want to get struck off Sir John and Lady Wilton's guest list at the British Embassy. I think the French have also got the message because their embassy and community are quite stand-offish.

As ambassadors go, Sir John Wilton is not bad, and he makes very good satirical copy in the *Eye*.

SATURDAY

Interviewed Farouk Akdar, the oil spokesman. He reports to Sheikh Yamani, the charismatic Oil and Petroleum Minister, who so graciously poured me bowls of lukewarm soup at his recent house party at Taif, in the mountains, when his daughter was leaving for Cambridge University, after her father had married his second or third wife.

Farouk is charismatic, younger and fatter than Sheikh Yamani, and he articulates the OPEC argument very well indeed, clearly and confidently. To cut a long story short, his argument is that it's high time that the oil-producing countries got their pound of flesh for their oil, and that it is sheer hypocrisy for the West to complain, in view of the way in which it has been screwing the Arab and Third World for centuries. He cites the example of the British taking cotton out of Egypt at the point of a gun in the days of Empire and then selling it back to the Egyptians at five times the price! And he points out, with a contented smile, that history's boot is on the other foot at last.

His historical arguments are both rational and persuasive, but when it comes to the harsh politico-economic realities of today's world, that's another matter entirely, and OPEC countries may find that they do not have the West over a barrel for time immemorial as they would wish, if they push their luck too far.

The desert kingdom, in particular, needs Western military support and expertise in a precarious part of the world in which the kingdom is not exactly flavour of the month with all its Arabian neighbours – some of whom would invade it tomorrow if they thought they could get away with it – and it is perfectly obvious that US and Western countries are managing to claw back much of the extra money that they are paying for the inflated price of oil by making the Arabians pay through the nose for the imports that they must take from the West in order to modernise. So it's a vicious tit-for-tat circle. Not that the Arabians seem to notice or care very much, not least because they can live with rip-off prices, whereas the bigger Western populations and economies are finding it very hard to do so.

But can Arabian citizens live with US construction companies, for example, selling the desert kingdom five times more concrete than it needs for projects it does not understand? As a result of which, pavement kerbstones are five times higher and steeper than they need to be – making it quite a ball-breaking climb (especially for old people) to get on and off pavements when they walk through town. And then there are those concrete bus shelters that are built like wartime bunkers.

SUNDAY

Re-read Evelyn Waugh's *Scoop* this evening. What a brilliant novel it is, relevant still for its satire, not only on the media's relentless and hectic pursuit of spurious 'hot' news, but on the bogus pride that it takes in its so-called 'ace' reporters. How mischievous and perceptive of Waugh to have sent the media up in this extremely funny and good-humoured way back in 1938 (one year before my birth and the outbreak of World War II).

I laughed right throughout the evening reading the exploits of William Boot and I feel so much better as a consequence. No doubt I shall have a chuckle and a giggle throughout the remainder of the week as I recall parts of the text. One feels so 'enriched' by a good novel and most weekends are enrichment time for me in this part of the world.

But what would Waugh have made of television reporters and presenters today, with their crass questions and pompous posturing, striking their ridiculous attitudes for the camera? What a blundering, blinding farce and complete waste of time so much of it is, and how essential it is to see through the dross, not least with the aid of William Boot of the *Daily Beast*, with whom I instantly identify.

But what an absurdly anarchic and chaotic world Waugh's is. There can be no doubt that Waugh's work – I have read most of it, except for his travel books – is cruelly funny and right on target. What a master of mordant comedy he was, so urbane and sophisticated in his exposé of false attitudes and the vanity of human desires, so rapid in his changes of scene, and effective in his extensive use of dialogue. Of course, some readers do not like his two-dimensional caricatures, but they overlook their satirical purpose. Nor do they like his sombre

Catholicism and imperialism. I, too, could do without that. But which of us is perfect? And all novels should be judged by the prevailing standards of the historical period in which they are set. Evelyn Waugh is dated, but *Scoop* strikes me as being timeless. I wonder what Waugh would make of the desert kingdom today, with his distaste for progress and modern civilisation, not to mention his apparent racism and predictable dislike of 'lesser breeds'?

It's whites and Christians who are the lesser breeds here. Christians are not allowed to practise their faith or to sport any religious symbols, such as crosses round their necks, for example.

One needs a good laugh in this country and one certainly gets through a lot of books to pass the time.

MONDAY

The cooker in my kitchenette exploded this evening! Went up in flames. Just like that.

Something mysteriously wrong with the gas container and it cannot be repaired until tomorrow morning. It exploded as soon as I switched on the gas and put a match to it – much to my astonishment (and horror), because there was no prior smell of leaking gas. But I managed to switch it off fast and chuck some water over the flames, because it was only a mini-explosion, so not in the least devastating. But it gave me quite a shock. I'll just have to live on bananas, water and cups of coffee until it's fixed tomorrow. Had hoped to fry some eggs and bacon, with fried bread. Not to worry. 'Life is life,' as the Russians say.

Have been offered a posting in the capital city, with my own detached villa, enclosed garden and swimming pool. But I don't think I'll take it because the capital is even more boring and straight-laced than here. At least Jeddah is a seaport town with people from the outside world coming and going all the time. Whenever I have visited the capital previously, it has always struck me as a hostile and isolated place, with many more formal restrictions, spies and far fewer expatriates. It is the desert kingdom at its least cosmopolitan and at its most narrow-minded, forbidding and parochial. Of course, the seat of government and royal palaces are in the capital, so it is heavily policed. But no foreign embassies or ambassadors are allowed there, so goodness knows what they would make of an interfering journalist on their doorstep.

The tight-lipped and stern-faced capital likes to keep foreign ambassadors and the outside world at a safe and not very respectable distance, and whenever the British or any other ambassador wants to go there in order to talk to members of its government, or its royal family, they must first go cap in hand to the authorities and ask for permission, grovelling at the feet of some petty official. They cannot travel without a special permit – a visitor's visa! How on earth they can conduct diplomatic relations in such a restrictive, inward-looking, suspicious and unfriendly place is a mystery to one and all – the short answer is that they cannot. Even the desert kingdom's own government ministers and secretaries prefer to get out of the capital at the first opportunity. So they are more often to be seen behind their desks down here on the cosmopolitan coast, than inland at the seat of power. People are much more accessible and possibly more relaxed and open here. They seem to lighten up with the sea air. Since I have been here, I've had instant access to the Minsters for Oil, Industry, Finance and Transport, as well as to the mayor, millionaire businessmen and industrialists, not to mention foreign ambassadors and their diplomatic staff.

Clearly, this is the place to be, not the capital. So I think I'll serve the remainder of my time here with my collapsing bed and exploding cooker, preferring, as always, the devil I know. This is a very trying and nerve-racking place. Best to keep cool at all times. As it happens, I'm quite good at that, which is just as well, in the circumstances.

TUESDAY

Cooker fixed, so had the fried eggs today. I wish I could get some Worcester Sauce out here, but can't find it anywhere. I really wish that I had stayed in the hotel where I spent my first months here. It wasn't much of a hotel, but at least the sheets were clean, the bed refused to fall apart, the air-conditioning worked, and I did not have to worry about fixing cookers and things. The restaurant was adequate and my room was serviced. Pity about the male room service and cleaning staff trying to touch one up all the time! Very tiresome and annoying when they won't take no for an answer. Especially when they creep into one's room in the dark, in the middle of the night, on the pretext that they thought you called for room service. Doesn't make for a relaxed atmosphere. Too much hassle and far too sexually tense. A pity also about the ban on women working in or visiting hotels.

WEDNESDAY

Have applied for an exit visa for my return to London and final exit from this country. It is necessary to apply early because it takes the authorities so long to process the paperwork as Arabian staff crawl like snails all over the forms, carefully scrutinising every word. It's not that they have so many visas to process, as in other more popular countries, but that they spend so much time checking out applicants to make quite sure that they have been behaving themselves during their stay, and to see if there have been any black marks against them, real or imaginary. Probably the authorities need time to make up their minds whether they should, in fact, allow applicants to leave or return in future. Some applicants are refused exit visas, either because the authorities or their employers need them to stay longer to complete some work that is considered to be important, or because somebody has it in for them for some reason, and has something against them, so is determined to settle an outstanding grudge. In the latter case, applicants will have some explaining and pleading to do about supposedly having put a foot wrong in the past and, since the authorities are corrupt as well as inefficient, it is always possible for them to be bribed, for or against an applicant. They might decide to be *against* in the event of someone having a grudge against an applicant, and wanting to put a final spoke in his or her wheel to cause maximum inconvenience on their way out of the kingdom; but they could also be *for* in the case of a large hint being dropped in the direction of the applicant that a bribe is all that is required in return for a magic signature on the exit form. The word 'refused' is seldom used when exit visas are not granted. Applications are simply and mysteriously 'delayed'. One can be delayed forever in the desert kingdom!

Everything is controlled and rubber-stamped, not once, but several times, and generally for the sheer hell of it. Most people are under constant suspicion and life is made very difficult, not least for foreigners with whom Arabians love to play a feeble game of cat and mouse, taking great pleasure from keeping foreigners guessing and exercising some power over them. Before an exit visa is granted, it is customary for the authorities to advertise the fact that the application has been made. Advertisements to this effect appear in the Arabic and English-language newspapers, complete with a photograph of the applicant for identification purposes, and inviting anyone with any claims against him or her – including financial claims for outstanding debts – to contact the authorities before a certain date. Inevitably, false claims can always be made and this delays the exit process, but no stone is left unturned and no chances are taken. When the exit visa is finally granted, there is still the 'ordeal' at the airport to be faced, when passport control or police officers painstakingly search every item of hand luggage to ensure that airline passengers are not escaping with the crown jewels, or carrying any religiously offensive or 'dirty' books! The whole irritating process is a long yawn. Then comes the body search and this can be a perfect little nightmare when Arabian lesbians in passport control have been known to take women passengers into private cubicles and grope them, whilst Arabian homosexuals sometimes do likewise to male passengers. Special attention is, of course, paid to the hand and other luggage of journalists, both at check-in and passport control, and for this reason I have arranged for this diary and certain other documents to be smuggled out of the desert kingdom in the untouched diplomatic bag of a friendly Western ambassador, just in case the authorities should confiscate or object to it in any way. One cannot be too careful.

THURSDAY

I have sometimes wondered what has kept me going in the desert kingdom for so long. A year is a long time here. More like three or four years, in view of the painfully slow rate at which time moves in this part of the world, where there is hardly anything to do, or anywhere to go, and no culture to enrich the mind and exercise the emotions. No concert or other music, art galleries, museums, theatres, poetry, literature, libraries and so on. So why haven't I packed it all in and left as soon as I could get my hands on an exit visa? There is, of course, always the light at the end of the tunnel – in the form of a pot of tax-free gold to keep one going – but what else is it that has kept me going in the meantime, from day to day? What drives me? There are loved ones back in the UK, including dependants, but it requires more than love to keep one on track here.

Most people are not 'driven' in the desert kingdom. They are either dragged along by events, or slowly tugged and pulled by that old tortoise called time, which hardly ever notices them, or anything else for that matter. I think that what energises me and keeps me going, at the rate of knots, is the next story that I must write after the completion of the current one. It is the chase that keeps me going and I am mindful of Scheherazade who kept herself alive and kicking in the *Arabian Nights' Entertainments* by telling her husband a story, night after night, without revealing the climax until the following night, and thereby postponing her execution for *A Thousand and One Nights*, the original title of the tales. Having married a ruthless king who killed his many wives successively on the morning after their marriage, Scheherazade managed to save her life by the endless tales that she told, keeping him hot with an overwhelming desire for the next night and the following story that would top the previous one. What a clever girl. Queen of multiple orgasms, and stories!

In a way, I am not unlike Scheherazade, as I keep myself from throwing the towel in and ending it all, as I stay ahead of the game by pursuing and telling one story after another until, finally, I am free to go at the end of my contract, having used the telling of unfinished stories to keep me and my readers going. Even this diary has an element of 'read on' and 'watch this space' about it as I record stories yet to be finalised or told. For example, the ongoing saga of the boiled eggs during Ramadan, the forthcoming interviews with this person or that, the progress or lack of it of my application for an exit visa, what to do this weekend and the weekend after? The sixteenth-century framework of stories that kept Scheherazade going is working for me, too, in the latter twentieth century.

But there is one sense in which my storytelling is not in the least like hers. Many of the stories that I must tackle are potentially more likely to get me into trouble than keep me out of it! More likely to anger than to placate kings, and so cause them to declare 'off with his head' rather than granting a stay of execution. So I must tread with more care. Even so, like Scheherazade, I do take care to tell most if not all of my stories in such a carefully balanced way that enables me to succeed in keeping out of trouble, taking pains not to publish anything displeasing under my by-line, while at the same time discreetly removing my by-line from displeasing copy and feeding it to *Private Eye*, or the diary columns back in London, for publication under anonymous authorship. So I do live to tell another tale and survive another day.

It is strange to think that the *Arabian Nights* tales were compiled as long ago as 1548 – probably in Cairo – long before they were translated into French and English in the eighteenth and nineteenth centuries, but that, since then, no such tales have been told here in the desert kingdom, even though many of these Persian stories were of Arabian and probably Indian origin. In Britain, Chaucer's *Canterbury Tales* are alive and well to this day, as fresh as picked flowers, as indeed are so many other tales, yet in the desert kingdom the *Arabian Nights* and storytelling generally has died a death that is mourned by no one.

FRIDAY

Under the weather today, high temperature, etc. Slept all day.

SATURDAY

Ditto temperature. Drinking plenty of water and fruit juice.

SUNDAY

Ditto temperature, but it's coming down now.

MONDAY

Have found a back street café that defies prayer times by staying open while others in the land of the pure close shop and rush off to the mosque five times a day. Have not mentioned this before but I have been taking fruit juice and other glasses of non-alcoholic gloom there for several weeks now in this thirsty country. But today – shock, horror! – the religious police suddenly turned up without warning. I daresay someone informed on the Arabian patron. They marched into the café, wielding their batons like loonies, with maniacal grins on their dire faces, as they deliberately swept cans of juice and savoury snacks off shelves, as well as knocking things off the serving counter, before proceeding to thump table tops so hard that they vibrated fiercely and caused customers' drinks – cans and glasses – to bounce off the tables and land in their laps or on the floor. While the police trashed the café, customers fled in all directions, whereupon the police proceeded to upturn the tables, as I could see from looking over my shoulder as I ran off. I also saw them take the patron by the scruff of the neck and march him off, presumably to the police station. What his fate was, I know not, because I did not go back to enquire later, for fear of the café being, very likely, under surveillance from here on. No point in my becoming a marked man, in addition to the poor patron, after I was lucky enough to escape without being detained and cross-examined in the first place. No point in getting myself arrested as an accomplice to such a 'sinful' crime, particularly when I have an application for an exit visa in progress.

At other times, religious police patrol the streets searching for long-haired youths and boys who haven't been near a barber for months. As soon as they spot an offending youth with too much hair on his neck or head – beards are OK for young men – they just grab him by the ear and twist it all the way to the nearest barber shop, where they stand over him as the barber gives him a short back and sides, for which he must pay, of course. If the youth doesn't have the money on him, he is marched home to his parents who must pay on demand.

Religious police also look for Western women who are stupid enough to wear short skirts in the desert kingdom. I once saw a beautiful young woman having her legs whipped in a *souk* by the police, for revealing too much leg and thigh. It turned out that she was a Swedish nurse working in the desert kingdom and, after being publicly disgraced in this way, she was then deported back to Sweden as an undesirable alien Jezebel. In a country in which veiled native women are not allowed to show their 'sexually provocative' faces, it stands to reason that no other women will be allowed to show other sexually alluring parts of their bodies. Unlike their Arabian sisters, Western and other women coming here are permitted to show their faces, but all else must stay firmly under wraps. Arabian women are not even allowed to carry their photographs in their passports because their men – fathers, brothers and husbands – live in fear of strange men looking into their give-away and perhaps inviting eyes, for some emotional recognition or bond, for some optical message of sexual desire or secret intent that the women might conceivably enjoy. With no mug shots in their passports, Arabian women are not required to drop their veils and show their faces to passport control and customs men, to see if their faces match up. Arabian women have blank spaces where their passport photographs ought to be, as blank as their real-life faces and blanked-out libidos. This is not only insulting to women, but it poses a security problem for the authorities as well, because it is possible, of course, for men to travel in and out of the kingdom on false passports, masquerading as women who do not have to show their faces. And it is thought that too many criminals, political agitators, assassins and terrorists from abroad are coming and going with impunity, thanks to the desert kingdom's sexual taboo on Arabian women's faces.

TUESDAY

Put a whole load of washing into my local Chinese laundry today. Should have put it in over the weekend, but forgot to do so on account of having been busy writing so many things. But the laundry is very fast and efficient and the manager – a smiling and toothy Chinese with a loud and heavily accented voice – tells me, 'Don't worry, Mr Clew, I shall put you at top of queue, and all will be ready tonight, or first thing tomorrow morning at the latest. OK?'

'OK,' I reply, 'I know I can rely on you, Mr Chan.' And usually one can rely upon Mr Chan.

I go through a lot of clothes in the heat here. Not working in an air-conditioned office each day, or benefiting from air-conditioned cars to take me everywhere – because I must get out and about in the streets on foot, treading the same dusty pavements as the Arabian population, visiting so many of the local haunts, workplaces and shops in order to get a feel for the place – my wardrobe is not at all like that of other expatriates who, unlike journalists, do not need to get out into the streets all day, in amongst the natives. My large Peugeot estate car is fine for long desert journeys, and getting to and from the office first thing in the morning and last thing at night. But during the day, with so many visits to be made, and people to be met in narrow back streets, one is on foot most of the time, sweating profusely in the merciless sun. So one needs a change of clothes, perhaps twice during the day, and once in the cool of evening, into something more formal, although I tend to wander about naked in my apartment most of the time.

So my wardrobe is not like that of most expatriates. It's full of crumpled cheesecloth shirts that soak up the sweat; lightweight jeans that wear well and do not show the creases;

well-sprung, durable sandals with extra-soft leather tops that do not cut into the sensitive skin of my naked feet; short-peaked sea captain's hats of the Helmut Schmidt variety, that fit lightly but tightly on my head so as not to give me a headache or blow away in this windy seaport city in which I find myself, and with enough peak to keep the sun out of my eyes over my dark glasses; several pairs of dark glasses to keep the wind and dust, as well as the sun, out of my eyes; more formal, long-sleeved summer shirts and a few ties for evening wear, or receptions; loads of underpants; an excess of handkerchiefs to mop one's brow when one is not blowing the sand from one's nose; cotten socks for occasional evening wear; only two pairs of lightweight summer shoes; and only a couple of jackets and summer trousers to match, for formal occasions. It is necessary to think much more here than elsewhere about clothes in relation to climate (such a sweaty climate).

I also get through an awful lot of specially treated foot powder and spray, prickly heat powder, talcum powder, anti-deodorant, aftershave, towels, shampoos and soap. One uses more towels than usual, not only on account of the extra number of showers that are taken here, but also on account of too many power cuts occurring when under the shower and smothered in thick soap (as a result of some workman having accidentally put his pick-axe through a cable). When that happens, there is no water to rinse the soap from one's hairy body, so recourse to even more towels is the only answer.

WEDNESDAY

Declined yet another invitation to watch dirty videos this evening with some Arabian friends. They watch them for hours and have been on at me to join them, for months, even though I always say, 'Thanks, but no thanks.' Not being bookworms, open-air types or having any particular hobbies, a lot of Arabians watch videos round the clock, rather than watching their heavily censored television, which is truly awful. And many of the videos that they watch are soft and hard porn, smuggled into the kingdom by Arabian princes, along with the illegal alcohol that they are supposedly not allowed to drink. Some of the princes control an underground distribution network for retailing videos and booze and, because they are princes, neither the Arabian Customs nor police dare to bother them, turning their attention elsewhere to ordinary mortals instead. And because it is an open secret that the princes are dealing in videos and illegal booze, it is to them that ordinary and lesser mortals go to make their black-market purchases. Many of these mortals are comfortably off middle-class types who can easily afford to bribe the police to keep them off their backs, given that the police are not so upright and moral that they, too, do not want to watch the pornographic videos! By all accounts, randy young and old Arabian men strip off when they are watching these porn videos, masturbating themselves and each other during the sexually explicit scenes. Yuk!

Even some of the heterosexual Western journalists whose company I keep here are slowly turning to homosexuality in the absence of women, and I once left a party in a fellow journalist's apartment where Western journalists, listening and swinging to jazz and pop music, could contain themselves no longer, so suddenly sprang to their feet and started to dance with one another, to my mild horror and utter astonishment! I was out of there like a bullet from a gun, leaving male journos from

Newcastle, Wolverhampton, Belfast, Manchester and London to dance together like girls. Not my cup of tea, I'm afraid.

Don't get me wrong. I have nothing against homosexuality between consenting adults, if that's what turns consenting adults on. But it simply doesn't appeal to me. It's a turn-off, not a turn-on, so forget it. I am not a prude or in any way repulsed. It's just that I do not warm to the idea, which doesn't do anything for me. I adore women and lust after them far too much to want to replace them with boys or men. In the absence of women, I prefer to comfort myself.

Some of the Arabian boys here openly look for sugar daddies, making themselves up with pretty, girlish faces and smiles, and some Western men that I know, who are not homosexuals, but are desperate for sex, are adopting the Arabian habit and giving the young boys a try. Some married Arabian men, who have entered into arranged marriages with wives with whom they are not sexually compatible, take houseboys in addition to their wives, just as their wives conduct lesbian affairs, secretly and otherwise, with other Arabian women.

The sex scene here is well and truly fucked up. By any standards and from all points of view, it could not be worse. Young Arabian boys and older men go hand in hand in public and without a murmur from the religious police. Arabian women openly hold all-female house parties and soirées with the approval of their husbands who drive their wives and daughters to the parties and then collect them afterwards. Women smooch, dance and flirt with each other at these parties.

THURSDAY

I think I'll read *The French Lieutenant's Woman* this weekend. It's one of the few remaining books that I have with me that I have not yet read.

God knows, I've read tons of books since I've been here. Let's see if I can remember some of them: *Arabian Sands* and the *Marsh Arabs* by Wilfred Thesiger; *Seven Pillars of Wisdom* and *Revolt in the Desert* by TE Lawrence; *Philby of Arabia* by Elizabeth Monroe; *The Arabs in History* by Bernard Lewis; The Penguin Classics *Tales from the Thousand and One Nights*; Chaucer's *Canterbury Tales*; Shakespeare's *Sonnets*; WH Auden's *Collected Poems*; Philip Larkin's *Collected Poems*; *The Diplomats* by Geoffrey Morehouse; *The White Nile* by Alan Morehead; *Oil Sheikhs* by Linda Blandford; *The History of Western Civilisation* and *Has Man a Future?* by Bertrand Russell; *Scoop* and *The Sword of Honour Trilogy* by Evelyn Waugh; and the first two of twelve novels, comprising one million words, in *A Dance to the Music of Time* by Anthony Powell, the remainder of which I am determined to read on my return to London. I cannot remember any more.

The Swedish Ambassador tells me that he is a crime writer in Sweden where he publishes murder mysteries. Perhaps he arranges for the fictional murder of politicians and diplomatic colleagues who get on the wrong side of him!

There are some very interesting people out here. The British and American Embassies have more Arabists than others, with the French in third place, while the Germans, Swedes and other Europeans seem to have no Arabists at all. While it must be very useful to have diplomats who are fluent in Arabic and able, therefore, to understand the Arabian culture, their linguistic abilities do not seem to win any more trade deals and contracts for their respective countries. Neither the British nor the French, for example, win more business because they have more embassy staff speaking Arabic. On the contrary, the USA, with fewer Arabists than the British, gets a much bigger slice of the cake, as do the Germans. Clearly, contracts are being awarded for political reasons or on grounds of unbeatable product quality, rather than an ability to speak to Arabians in their own tongue. Some people say that Arabians are suspicious of foreigners who speak Arabic, believing them to be spies, and definitely not liking the idea of foreigners being able to understand what Arabians are saying. Obviously, it's easier to keep foreigners in the dark if they don't understand what is being said.

FRIDAY

Read John Fowles' *French Lieutenant's Woman*.

What a masterly and lucid *tour de force* this novel is about how it actually *feels* to defy the social tyrannies. A persistent yet gentle *tour de force* and with such astonishing clarity.

And what a clear insight into sexual repression. Most enjoyable.

Fowles is so intelligent and philosophical – and what a fine and masterful textual density and complexity he has woven, but with such a light touch, in his respect for nature and individual freedom.

I like his existential emphasis on the need for independent self-realisation and the clear recognition that hazard plays in even the best-planned lives. He is such a brilliant storyteller, too. I have been reading the book, on and off, all day. It is *such* a joy.

I find his characters very compelling and I love the vivid social context in which he sets them. As for the enigmatic nature of sexual relations, I think that he deals with it very well indeed. There is such a clear and fascinating recognition of *the eternal problem* of individual sexual freedom and the desire of others to manipulate and control that freedom, and what to do about it?

I think that every young man and woman in the desert kingdom should be required to read this novel. It should become essential reading. Some hope.

But this country is full of sexually repressed women who live in constant fear of the social tyrannies and sexual taboos – few of whom defy them for fear of being stoned to death!

The desert kingdom is full of potential French Lieutenants' women, in one way or another, but few who will grasp the nettle.

Good night, Mr Fowles.

SATURDAY

Had a surprise visit today from two young Arabian women in Western clothes. They wore jeans and open-necked shirts, and looked somewhat like gypsies with dirty faces and wild eyes. They rang my apartment doorbell – unaccompanied women are not supposed to visit men in their apartments – and boldly asked if they could use my shower! Just like that. They came out with it, these two women whom I did not know from Adam – or should it be Eve? – and whom I had never set eyes on before. I could not believe my ears or my eyes. Needless to say, I was not only astonished, but also highly suspicious, and somewhat at a loss to know whether or not I should oblige them. The thought crossed my mind that perhaps the religious police were using them to set Western men up – especially those who had applied for exit visas. But given that Arabian women are not allowed to go out in Western clothes and without their veils, I quickly decided that this was probably not the case. On the other hand, they were Arabian, weren't they? So what was going on here and were they not taking a hell of a risk, dressed as they were? Who on earth were they, for heaven's sake? They were attractive enough, but where had they come from, and why were they so wild-eyed? They looked desperate and in need of a shower, no doubt about it, so I invited them in for further questioning, quickly closing the door behind them before any Arabian neighbours spotted them at my door.

They explained that they were Palestinian refugees who were roughing it in the desert kingdom. I was puzzled to hear this, because Palestine is not exactly just down the road from here, and I am not aware that the desert kingdom is in the habit of letting Palestinian women cross its borders and roam its streets. On the other hand, they may have strayed into the kingdom, and they certainly looked as though they had been roughing it somewhere for some purpose or other. Maybe they had fallen into the hands of slave traders and had managed to escape from one of their brothels. Maybe they were on the run from one of the desert kingdom's jails. Because their English wasn't that good, apparently, there was a limit to the questions that they could answer satisfactorily, so I finally elected to be done with it and let them use my shower.

When they were dressed, they told me that they were starving because they had not eaten for more than 24 hours, so I fed them as well, and soon discovered that they certainly were hungry, as they fell like vultures on every morsel. After they had eaten, they kissed me on both cheeks and went on their way. It is the first and only time that I have had women in my apartment, something which is generally unheard of in the desert kingdom where women are too scared to take such risks.

SUNDAY

How clever of Mr Fowles to have recreated a Victorian romance in a modern setting and with such a contemporary twist.

I love these open endings in novels. Reading this novel, one is learning as much about the nature of fiction as the nature of life. There is an endlessly fascinating interaction between reality and history, and a fundamental concern with the uncertainty of existence that is reflected in the use of the open ending.

I must read more of John Fowles in future. I have seen the film, but not read the novel before, and both have proved to be such a pleasure.

Feeling rather nostalgic today, I also read Auden's *Night Mail*, which is a poem to make one feel homesick in this country, where there are no trains or railway stations. Rich and poor travel across the kingdom by aeroplane or camel – and otherwise along desert motorways in cars and lorries – which is how the mail is delivered likewise (when it is delivered at all, that is!).

Against this background, Auden's poem tugs at the heart. But there is no night mail here, as Auden would have understood it.

Neither is there any evidence of too many cheques or postal orders in circulation. To judge from the long queues outside the banks – where rich oil sheikhs drag huge sacks and polythene bags full of thousands of pounds' worth of notes along the pavements behind them, while they wait to get inside the counting houses – it is clear that the vast majority of domestic financial transactions are still done with coinage and paper money. Once inside, the sheikhs empty the contents of their sacks on to the counters and then wait patiently while the Arabian bank clerks count them. Certainly, most employers pay their staff in cash, counting out hundreds of notes to them in bulk each month, which the employees then tie up in their handkerchiefs and carry around with them for days, before they can find a bank without a queue, where they can pop in and deposit their salaries. Hardly ever does anyone get robbed, burgled or mugged at the sight of so much money being carried around in public – and left in parked cars – which is perhaps hardly surprising in view of the fact that thieves have their hands chopped off for such crimes. Banks do not get broken into, as far as anyone can tell.

MONDAY

Yet another British lorry driver in prison here. Decided to visit him and take him some groceries from the supermarket to cheer him up.

Whenever foreign lorry drivers are involved in a road accident, however minor, the Arabian police instantly send them to jail. They do not ask questions, but automatically assume that foreign drivers are to blame when, most of the time, they are not. The first time that I wrote about a British driver who had been wrongly and needlessly put behind bars, questions were asked in the House of Commons in London, the first ever to be tabled about the fate of British lorry drivers here. This was a real pain to British diplomats here who would rather not be bothered, thank you very much. They have their minds on higher things.

I was also asked by the lorry driver's local newspaper – the *Lancashire Evening Post* – to interview and profile the driver, which I did, and following the questions raised by British MPs back in London, pressure was put on the British Embassy in Jeddah to kindly pull its finger out, which it is not accustomed to doing.

One reason why the Arabian police immediately side with locals against foreign drivers is because, under the law, blood money must be paid by those who inadvertently kill others in road and other accidents. So, if the police report that accidental deaths to Arabians were the fault of foreign drivers, then it is the foreigners who must pay up, lining the pockets of the locals. And even when no one is killed or injured in a road accident, the police take an all too obvious delight in putting foreigners behind bars to teach them a lesson and remind them that they are unwelcome infidels! Such is the nature of the enormous inferiority complex of the desert kingdom.

Blood money is something to the order of 18 camels (or an equivalent value) for the death of an Arabian man, and nine for the death of an Arabian woman. Most British and other foreign lorry drivers haven't a clue how much a camel costs, and they cannot afford to pay the bloody money, so they must look to their employers to shell out, in order to get them out of jail. But if small company employers are not insured, they cannot always come up with the money. So there is a real problem that is distressing to a significant number of lorry drivers and to their families back in Britain.

The driver whom I visited today was very pleased to see me and he told me that I spent much longer with him – one hour

– than the diplomat from the British Embassy ... ten minutes. No wonder I am a thorn in their flesh. He also described the filthy and harsh conditions in the jail, of which I was already aware, of course – overcrowded and extremely hot, small cells infested with rats, ants and cockroaches, filthy and unhygienic loos, having to sleep on stone floors, disgusting and inedible food, and brutal and mentally deranged jailers who think nothing of beating or torturing prisoners, especially if they are white, for their own amusement when they are not sexually assaulting or raping the male and female inmates. The stench in the jails is dreadful and some poor prisoners – locals and Westerners – have been left to rot in them for years rather than months. These could be political prisoners, fraudsters, people in debt, people whose faces do not fit, people dealing in or drinking illegal alcohol, serious criminals, and so on.

TUESDAY

Had an urgent request to go back to the jail today and visit my lorry driver again. I thought he was perhaps going to tell me that he was being beaten or tortured already.

But it transpired that he wanted to inform me of a rumour going round the jail that a British bulldozer driver, who was imprisoned there, had committed suicide.

I knew of the driver in question. He had committed suicide. I was not as shocked as others to hear this, because it is a well-kept secret that foreigners and others sometimes commit suicide in Arabian jails. But I was depressed to hear it.

I thanked my lorry driver for alerting me to this rumour and told him that I would look into it, while also keeping an eye on his welfare, badgering the embassy and continuing to visit him so that his jailers could see that he was not abandoned or forgotten by the outside world.

When I got on the phone to the British Embassy, they did not deny the rumour. They had been informed, they said, by the Arabian authorities, so I immediately filed a story.

The Embassy also told me that my lorry driver, who was innocent and had been wrongfully imprisoned, would be released tomorrow. So I returned at once to the jail to let him know that the rumour was correct and to tell him that he would be out the next day.

He told me that he had seen some bloodstained prisoners who were black and blue as a result of having been beaten, and others who could hardly walk because the soles of their feet had been systematically thrashed by jailers.

He also said that he would personally like to get his hands round the necks of some of the jailers and strangle them in a slow and painful death. I replied that, while this was a splendid idea, it was best to keep cool, swallow one's pride and get out of there with all possible speed.

WEDNESDAY

OK, so today is prediction time. I have been thinking ahead, looking ahead and trying to predict how much change – real hand on heart change, not cosmetic alteration and outward-appearance change – is likely to have taken place here in the desert kingdom in, say, 25 years' time?

A quarter of a century seems a reasonable length of time in which to give the desert kingdom a chance to change. So, come the new millennium, when the rest of the world – the outside world – moves on, forward into a new century, how much of the dire backwardness of this stick-in-the-sand country will have moved on with it, as opposed to having remained stubbornly unchanged at heart?

How much will have changed for the better or at all? While things will obviously have been modernised, will there have been a change of heart and mind? Will this undemocratic desert kingdom have undertaken social and electoral reforms? I doubt it. But we shall have to wait and see. In the meantime, here are my predictions. The following lists represent the changes that probably will and will not have taken place by the new millennium.

PROBABLE CHANGES

- Change will no longer be regarded as 'the spoiling finger of time', as Thesiger termed it.
- Fewer people will live in tents and mud huts.
- There will be many more modern housing estates and private villas with pools.
- Regular power cuts will hopefully be a thing of the past.
- There will be fewer water shortages.
- There will be many more hospitals and health will have improved.
- There will be more home comforts.
- Streets will be named at last.
- Backlogs of mail may no longer be burned.
- No more filthy loos, perhaps, and no more peeing on the roof.
- Pot-holed roads will be brought up to world-class standards.
- There will be many more cars, road vehicles and domestic air services.

- Pavements will be paved and the streets will no longer be strewn with garbage.
- Skyscrapers will have made their mark on the desert landscape.
- There will be much more air-conditioning.
- The desert kingdom's industry, distribution and transportation networks will be properly structured.
- There will be far fewer cash transactions as more cheques and postal orders circulate.
- The desert kingdom may not continue to have the Western world over a barrel on account of oil (which will continue to be a weapon, but possibly less powerful).
- The desert kingdom will no longer be as rich as it was during the first flush of its petro-dollars in the 1970s, but the rich will, of course, get richer still.
- Arabian women will eventually be required to carry their photographs in their passports (if only for reasons of national security).
- Some (but not many) Arabian women will be able to go to university and out to work.
- There will be less incompetence and inefficiency, but not much less.
- Bottles of water and apple juice ('desert kingdom champagne') will be much cheaper.
- Foreign ambassadors will be let out of quarantine and allowed into the capital city at last without having to go cap in hand to the Arabian Government for special permission.
- The British Ambassador, Sir John Wilton, will have gone into retirement, having become famous for a column being named after him in *Private Eye*.
- Exit and entrance visas may possibly be easier to acquire and

quicker to process, without the requirement of a Certificate of Religion to prove that you are not a Jew or an Atheist.

PROBABLE RESISTANCE TO CHANGE

- Arabian women will still have to wear the veil.
- They will still be stoned to death for committing adultery.
- Most Arabian women will not be able to go to university or out to work.
- There will still be sexual apartheid and segregated beaches.
- Homosexuality and lesbianism will continue to be rampant.
- Public beheadings will continue to be a popular blood sport.
- Thieves will still have their hands chopped off.
- People will continue to be flogged in public.
- The police and taxi drivers may still be slapping non-Muslim faces from the Third World.
- Foreigners may still be forbidden to eat in work and public places during Ramadan.
- Food in restaurants and hotels will not have improved very much.
- Christians and other non-Muslims will still be forbidden to practise their religions in public places in the desert kingdom and to wear or display non-Muslim religious symbols.
- Booze will continue to be illegal.
- There will still be pubs and hotels with no beer.
- *Sidiki* will continue to be in demand on the black market.
- The press will continue to be heavily censored.
- Corruption will continue.

- There will continue to be no railways or railway stations.
- Jails will still be filthy, rat-infested places where tortures are flavour of the month.
- There will be hardly any electoral or social change worthy of the name.
- The royal family will continue to dominate and set the tone.
- Foreigners will very probably have to carry their passports with them at all times.
- The *Arabian Nights* and Chaucer's *Canterbury Tales* will always be a delight to read!

Why do people keep diaries? Why do others read their diaries? They keep them in order not to forget what they cannot possibly imagine or remember in the fullness of time, in order to record the dates and the detail, in order to have a daily record of events, thoughts and feelings, in order to work things out in their own psyche and to have a dialogue with themselves about what is going on in their lives, in order to make a careful note of history. And they write their diaries for themselves alone, unless they are politicians who write their diaries with an eye to publication and making big bucks, and for political or propaganda purposes, fashioning history to their own ends, and with a certain audience in mind, in which case the diarist is talking not only to himself, but addressing imagined readers as well. Such diaries are more suspect and less innocent than others.

It stands to reason that diaries that are written with an eye to publication will be written differently from others and perhaps more self-consciously. But why am I writing this diary? I will pursue this question tomorrow ... too tired tonight. Good night, diary.

THURSDAY

I am writing this diary because so much has happened to me in such a short space of time in the desert kingdom, the extraordinary detail of which seems to me quite mind-blowing and of some historical significance. Maybe I can get this diary published some day. Maybe not. In which case, let it gather dust in my attic. But if I do, let readers understand that I am writing this diary for myself – the best of all possible motives – and not for them.

But why do people want to read other people's diaries? To study them? To share an experience with them? To travel with them? To pry into their affairs and private lives? To gain access to useful information? To gain access to 'off record' information that is not otherwise available? To live their lives through others? To admire the diarist's art? To widen their circle of friends? To escape? To keep the company of a diarist for a change? Why not? They are all valid reasons.

But whatever their reasons, those who read diaries should never forget that a diary is selective and inevitably subjective. Much is left out for reasons of space, time and, not least, preference, and that which is kept in is written in a hurry and on the run, either at the sleepy end of a day, or throughout the day in short bursts. It is also important to remember that some people are more truthful with themselves than others, just as some people are more keenly observant and capable of packing more things into their diaries than others. Such diaries will therefore have greater range and depth.

Some diarists are more concerned about certain things, and dwell upon them accordingly, so they will not necessarily record absolutely everything that has happened to them, and what they record is only their version of events and not, of course, the word of God ... thank God! Even so, unless diarists are absolute fantasists, he or she has an important truth to tell, as they see it, and can be given the benefit of the doubt on that basis.

Some diaries are written as a form of daily therapy for the diarist who has much to get out of his or her system, while others skip the therapy and stick to the facts, keeping the emotions at arm's length and leaving feeling for another day. Some are heavy with emotion and streams of consciousness, whilst others are more balanced. Some diaries have a better sense of humour than others.

But, however a diary is written, and for whatever reason, it is a mental discipline as demanding as physical press-ups for keep-fit purposes each day, which is why a lot of people cannot be bothered, and who can blame them? There are also diaries that run out of steam, alas, either because not enough is happening to the diarist, or because what is happening is too tedious for words and contains too much packing.

On such occasions, it is better for the diarist to leave some blank pages entitled 'watch this space'. Better to remember that paper is patient, so a diarist can take his or her time. It is, after all, a diary that is being written, not a daily newspaper with tight deadlines and a publisher thumping the desk.

FRIDAY

This has been a quiet week. Not much happening. Nothing unusual about that for most Arabians. They go through their slow lives without anything much happening most of the time and they seem to have resigned themselves to it. They work at a snail's pace in the mornings, keeping out of the blistering sun, and in the shade as much as possible, and then they sleep during the exceedingly hot afternoons before taking a leisurely stroll in the cooler evenings. Heat exhaustion is a real problem here.

There is not much of a 'social whirl' to get most Arabians out of their high-walled villas and houses, so they just sit around and eat a lot, and make small talk. Some smoke their *hookah*s, whilst others are endlessly drinking small cups of sweet and sickly Arabian tea. Others hang around street corners and in *souk*s, lifting the bottom ends of their ankle-length *thobe*s and flapping them around their knees in order to encourage a draft to cool the insides of their hot thighs. With common consent, it is a familiar sight to see fat Arabian men talking to each other at street corners, flapping the bottom ends of their *thobe*s with one hand, while picking their noses with the other! But most do not go anywhere unless they really have to, because it is so painfully hot here, bitterly hot.

It's the expatriates who make things happen, undertaking safaris and making their own entertainment inside their compounds and houses, while the Arabians stay at home most of the time, in their un-happening lives. And the Arabians think nothing of turning up hours or days late for business appointments, not because they are so busy and overstretched, but because they cannot get their act together, cannot get into the mood or right frame of mind for facing people, because they do not feel sufficiently disciplined or accountable. Sometimes it is necessary to go back, day after day, to keep an appointment with an Arabian who forgot to turn up. They have a saying in the desert for people who turn up late – 'the traveller has his own excuses' – but the majority of Arabians in this seaport town are certainly not travellers, by any stretch of the imagination. They couldn't 'travel' from one end of town to the other, most of them. But nobody's fussed. It's the way things are and have always been.

But, for me, it is very unusual to have not much happening, because I have to chase or find newspaper stories all the time, interviewing so many different people of all nationalities, and paying attention to their babble, without nodding off in the process, without getting involved or taking sides, without losing my concentration and sense of purpose, without losing my inspiration to go off and write it all down, and this suits me just fine.

I think the reason why there has not been much happening for me this week is because I busted a gut at the beginning of the week and got so far ahead of myself that I finished all my stories in double-quick time, so this week I have not been struggling like others with unfinished stories to complete. In the meantime, no new stories have come up, for some reason, which is unusual, so I am in the happy position of being able to take a breather. On the other hand, it doesn't do to have nothing to do in this place, *because there really is nothing to do*, and one can quickly become very bored or depressed, and finish up like the Arabians, lethargic, dejected and purposeless. I cannot take myself off to an art gallery, cinema, stage, theatre, wine bar, club or pub, as I could do back home. I cannot go for a drive into the lush countryside or for a walk in the park. So I like having a lot to do here in order to keep my mind off how little I like this dull place, which really is nothing to write home about, and has, truth to tell, so little to recommend it.

SATURDAY

Spent an interesting evening with an Arabian friend and his wife. He is by far the nicest Arabian I know and it is always a pleasure to keep his company. He is a gentle, civilised soul, with a good sense of humour, and always laid back. I like his style, probably because, in these respects, he is not unlike me. He has had the benefit of a good education and his young wife is not so well educated, but she is not uneducated and is always very charming. He is lucky enough to have travelled widely – Europe, United States, India and the Far East – so he has a good global perspective on life and people and he is not without money, of course, unlike me. His is one of the more powerful, albeit quietly understated families in the desert kingdom, and he has certainly proved to be a very good friend and 'minder' to me, getting me out of trouble from time to time. One is lost without a minder here – with a powerful family on your side, you can get away with a good many things, and escape with a caution, but not otherwise.

A lot of Arabian men keep their wives, sisters and daughters locked away in parts of their houses where they cannot be seen by male visitors, and should these women show their faces at all they are required to know their place and wear their veils. But my friend and others like him are much more liberal-minded and entertain visitors at home in the company of their unveiled wives. My friend's most amusing habit is to play with his worry beads when the pressure is on, with a big smile on his face which suggests that he is not worried at all and that the beads are a complete waste of time! I know that he thinks that most conventions and human vanity are a waste of time and that most people are a big bore.

Let's hope my exit visa comes through on time. No news as yet.